HISTORY IN DEPTH

# JAPA
# THE MODERN

*For my mother and father*



First published 1989

Published by
MACMILLAN EDUCATION LTD
Houndmills, Basingstoke, Hampshire RG21 2XS
and London
Companies and representatives
throughout the world

Printed in Hong Kong

British Library Cataloguing in Publication Data
Wilmot, Eric
Japan in the modern world.——(History
in depth).
1. Japan, 1900–1984
I. Title II. Series
952.04
ISBN 0–333–46359–5

# CONTENTS




## *Acknowledgements*

The author and publishers wish to thank the following who have kindly given permission for the use of copyright material:

The Athlone Press for extracts from *Showa: An Inside History of Hirohito's Japan* by Tessa Morris-Suzuki, copyright © Tessa Morris-Suzuki 1984; The International Institute for Strategic Studies for a table from *The Military Balance 1879–80* by H. Kitamura; Japanese Ministry of Foreign Affairs for material from *The Japan of Today*, 1980; McGraw-Hill Book Company for material from *Sources of Japanese History, Vol. 2* by David John Lu, 1974; Methuen & Co. for an extract from *Japan Advances* by Prue Dempster, 1967; Reuters for an extract from a 1954 press report; Times Newspapers Ltd. for extracts from various editions of *The Times*.

The author and publishers wish to acknowledge, with thanks, the following photographic sources:

BBC Hulton Picture Library pp7 top, 7 centre, 7 bottom, 9, 13, 17 right, 22 (Bettmann Archive), 25 bottom (Bettmann Archive), 54, 58; Camera Press pp21, 34; Mary Evans Picture Library p6; Kyodo News Enterprise pp24 left, 27, 31, 33 right, 50, 51 left, 52; Popperfoto pp5, 17 top, 17 left, 24 right, 25 top, 33 left, 36, 39, 41, 43, 48, 53, 56 left, 56 right, 57.

The publishers have made every effort to trace the copyright holders, but if they have inadvertently overlooked any, they will be pleased to make the necessary arrangements at the first opportunity.

# PREFACE

The study of history is exciting, whether in a good story well told, a mystery solved by the judicious unravelling of clues, or a study of the men, women and children whose fears and ambitions, successes and tragedies make up the collective memory of mankind.

This series aims to reveal this excitement to pupils through a set of topic books on important historical subjects from the Middle Ages to the present day. Each book contains four main elements: a narrative and descriptive text, lively and relevant illustrations, extracts of contemporary evidence, and questions for further thought and work. Involvement in these elements should provide an adventure which will bring the past to life in the imagination of the pupil.

Each book is also designed to develop the knowledge, skills and concepts so essential to a pupil's growth. It provides a wide, varying introduction to the evidence available on each topic. In handling this evidence, pupils will increase their understanding of basic historical concepts such as causation and change, as well as of more advanced ideas such as revolution and democracy. In addition, their use of basic study skills will be complemented by more sophisticated historical skills such as the detection of bias and the formulation of opinion.

The intended audience for the series is pupils of eleven to sixteen years; it is expected that the earlier topics will be introduced in the first three years of secondary school, while the nineteenth and twentieth century topics are directed towards first examinations.

# 1 THE RISING SUN

## *Earthquake!*

According to legend, in a deep and hidden ocean beneath Japan, there lived a gigantic catfish. When angered by the foolishness of the people above, he would heave his back in rage, causing the land to buckle and split open. At midday on 1 September 1923, the catfish stirred. The cities of Tokyo and Yokohama were rocked by the terrifying force of a massive earthquake. Hundreds of buildings crashed to the ground, killing and injuring scores of people. Most of the movement ceased after about five minutes, only to be replaced by another, more deadly peril – fire. Amidst the wreckage of people's homes, smouldering charcoal burners which had been lit in preparation for the midday meal began to set fire to the shattered timber structures. Within hours the cities were ablaze. The fires lit the evening sky and could be seen 160 kilometres away. In this fearsome inferno 140 000 people were burned to death. By the time the fires were put out, two-thirds of Japan's capital city lay in ruins, but the devastation was even greater at Yokohama, where hardly a building was left standing. This was one of Japan's worst natural disasters. Some older and more superstitious Japanese people saw the earthquake as punishment for half a century of modernisation and progress. The catfish, they believed, had been roused because the ways of old Japan were gradually being replaced by new and 'dangerous' ideas from the West.

*Tokyo: aftermath of the 1923 earthquake*

Commodore Perry's naval expedition to Japan, 1853

## *Modern Japan*

From the mid-seventeenth century, Japan had followed a policy known as Sakoku, meaning 'closed country', and had deliberately isolated itself from any contact with the West. Then, in July 1853, four American warships commanded by Commodore Matthew C. Perry entered Tokyo harbour. The Commodore carried with him a letter from the President of the United States, Millard Fillmore, requesting a trade treaty between the two countries. The following year a treaty was signed and similar arrangements were soon made with Britain, Russia and Holland. From this point on, the doors of Japan were opened ever wider to the influence of the West.

At the time of Perry's historic visit to Japan, the country was ruled by the Shogun, the Emperor's military deputy, a position which had been in the hands of the Tokugawa family since 1603. However, the power of the Shogun was now in decline and in 1868 the authority of the Emperor was restored. Under the Emperor Meiji, Japan modernised rapidly. Heavy industry began to be developed and trade with the West increased. Communications and transport were improved with the construction of an extensive railway network and the introduction of a telephone and telegraph system. Everywhere the influence of the West could be seen; foreign advisers are estimated to have given the Meiji government a total of 9500 man-years of service. With their guidance a modern army was trained and equipped, based on French and German models, and the navy was developed along British lines. Schools based on Western practices were opened, and in 1889 a new constitution which borrowed heavily from Germany was proclaimed.

The Meiji period also brought great changes to everyday life. Western-style dress became very popular, and the ancient practice of carrying swords was dropped. In the major cities, gas lamps lit the streets and electric tramways provided efficient public transport. Even the traditional Japanese diet was affected as beef, apples, coffee, tea and beer were introduced and tasted for the first time by many people.

## *Using the evidence: the transformation of Japan*

A *Tokyo in 1905*

B *Japanese diplomats in Paris, 1862*

C *Japanese government officials in 1877*

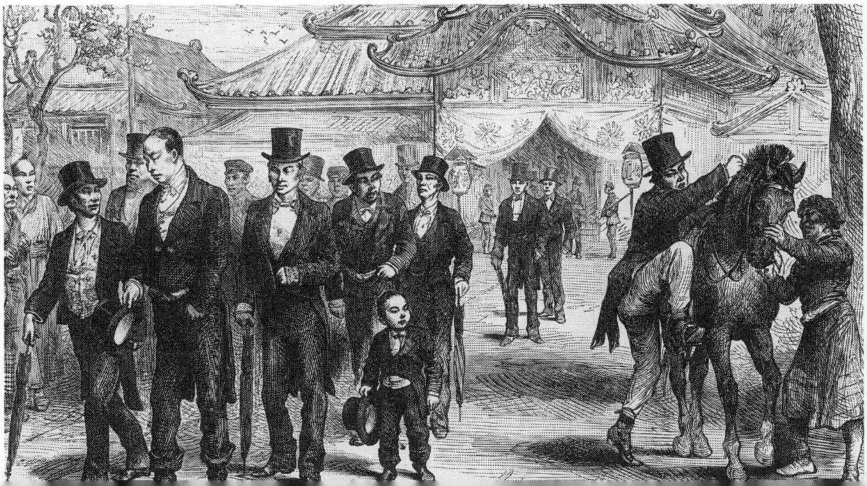

D *Sir George Sansom refers to a popular children's song, composed in 1878, known as the 'Civilization Ball Song', in which children counted the bounces of a ball, reciting ten desirable Western objects – gas lamps, steam-engines, horse carriages, cameras, telegrams, lightning-conductors, newspapers, schools, letter-post and steam-boats.*

Richard Storry: *A History of Modern Japan*, 1960

1 Examine source **A** closely. What evidence can you find to support the claim that by 1905 Tokyo had become a modern city?

2 Sources **B** and **C** show Japanese government officials. What differences do you notice in their appearance? How would you account for these differences?

3 a) Look again at source **D**. How might the following items listed in the song have contributed to the modernisation of Japan?
   (i) gas lamps;
   (ii) steam-engines;
   (iii) telegrams;
   (iv) steam-boats.
b) If you were to compose a 'Civilization Ball Song' today, which ten items would you include?

---

## *The Russo-Japanese War*

If there were any doubts about Japan's ability to stand alongside other world powers, they were soon forgotten in 1904–5 when the army and navy took on and defeated the mighty Russian Empire. Trouble between the two countries flared up over rival claims to influence in Korea and Manchuria (an extensive region of China). In 1900, during the Boxer Rebellion in China, Russia had moved large numbers of troops into Manchuria to protect the railway line which gave them access to the important seaports of Vladivostok, Port Arthur and Dairen. This sort of action alarmed the Japanese, who were determined to prevent the extension of Russian control into an area which they considered to be a Japanese sphere of influence. It was not long before the antagonism between the two powers erupted into full-scale war. On 8 February 1904, the Japanese navy made a surprise torpedo attack on the Russian Asiatic Fleet while it lay at anchor in Port Arthur. This was followed by a blockade of the harbour, which kept the Russian fleet out of the way as thousands of Japanese soldiers landed in Korea. The army had the difficult task of capturing the Russian stronghold of Port Arthur, and they had to do so quickly. Russia had hastily dispatched its considerable Baltic Fleet to the scene of the fighting and every passing day brought it closer. The siege of Port Arthur cost the lives of thousands of men on both sides. According to the historian David Bergamini the slaughter was on a vast scale:

> *Wave after wave of Japanese advanced into withering fire and bewildering mine-fields. The no-man's-land before the fortress writhed with wounded who could not be helped. The stench of corpses hung so heavy on the air that the Russian defenders on the ramparts wore handkerchiefs soaked in camphor.*
>
> David Bergamini: *Japan's Imperial Conspiracy*, 1971

Despite the appalling conditions the Japanese captured Port Arthur and followed this up with another notable victory at Mukden in March 1905. The Russian Baltic Fleet arrived in May and was promptly annihilated as it attempted to pass through the Tsushima Strait, the cold waters of the Sea of Japan claiming the lives of some 12 000 Russian sailors.

The Treaty of Portsmouth which ended the war brought considerable gains to Japan. Russia was forced to give up the southern half of the island of Sakhalin and had to transfer her leases for the railway in Manchuria to Japanese possession. It was also agreed that Japan could establish a protectorate over Korea. However, the real significance of this episode was that it firmly established Japan as the leading power in East Asia and made her a force to be reckoned with in international affairs.

*The Russian flagship,* The Petropavlosk, *sinking off Port Arthur in 1904*

## *The growth of industry*

Japan's rapid progress towards becoming a major world power was further accelerated when she became involved in the Great War of 1914–18. Japan had begun to industrialise in the last quarter of the nineteenth century, but it was during the war that she really became an industrial power capable of challenging the rest of the world. At the beginning of the war Japan supported Britain, the country to which she had been allied since 1902, and declared war on Germany. This proved to be a very profitable move for the Japanese. Preoccupied with fighting the French, Russians and British in Europe, Germany was in no position to defend her Far Eastern interests adequately. Japan was therefore able to seize control of them, meeting little resistance. Perhaps more importantly, Japan was able to begin supplying markets which had previously relied upon the products of the great European powers. Countries such as India, Australia and China came to depend increasingly on the manufactures of Japanese industry. Shipbuilding and textiles were two concerns which benefited greatly from the war. When World War I ended in 1918, Japan had an export surplus of some 350 million yen.

*Using the evidence: industrialisation*

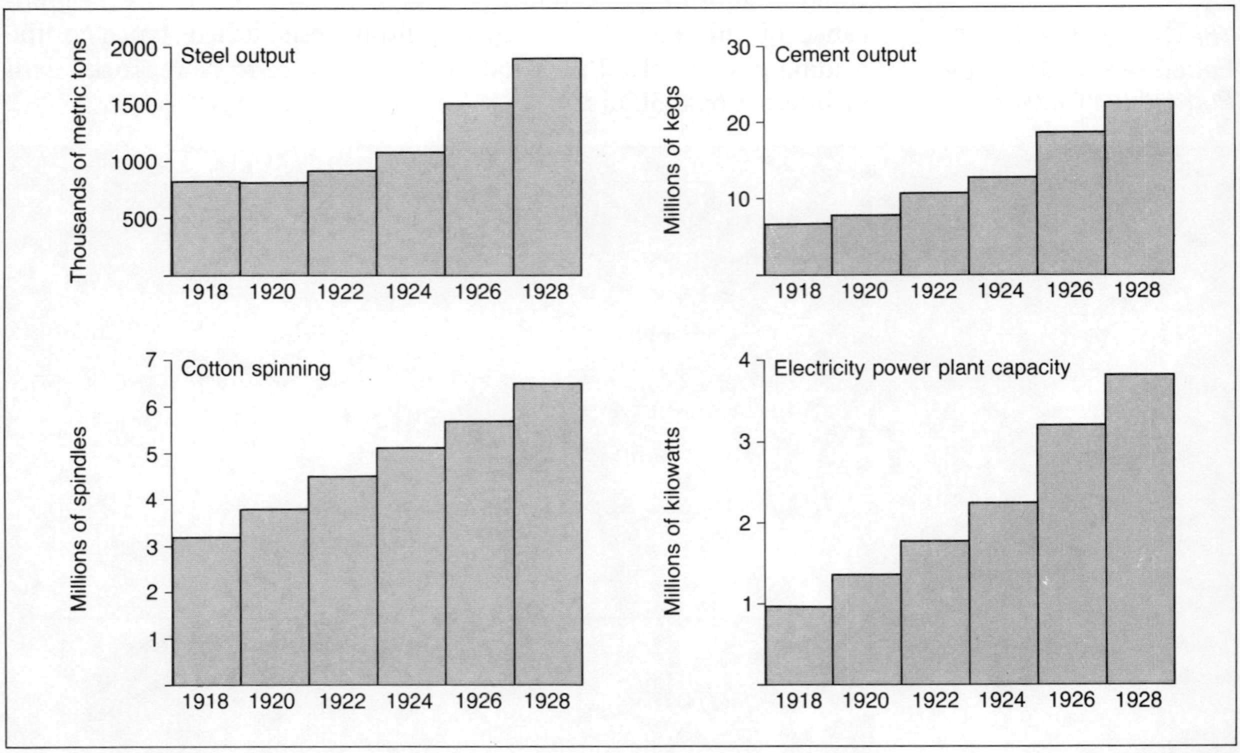


Graphs based on statistics in Harold Moulton's book, *Japan, an Economic and Financial Appraisal*, 1931.

1 By how much did output increase between 1918 and 1928 in:
   a) the steel industry;
   b) the cement industry?

2 Suggest ways in which the increased output of the cement industry might have been used to help the development of Japan as a modern, industrial nation.

3 Make a copy of the chart below. In the appropriate column list the ways in which the increased output of electricity (graph 4) could have benefited Japanese industry and the ordinary Japanese citizen.

| *Benefits for industry* | *Benefits for the citizen* |
|---|---|
| | |

4 Graph 3 shows the increase in the number of spindles used in the cotton spinning industry between 1918 and 1928. Does this information prove that the output of the cotton industry increased? Explain your answer.

5 Why would it be inaccurate to present these graphs as proof that by 1928 Japan had become a leading world industrial power? What additional information would you need in order to support that claim?

6 By the end of the 1920s Japan was still having to import considerable quantities of steel from abroad. How would you interpret graph 1:
   a) without this information;
   b) with this information?

7 In the light of your answers to question 6, what in your opinion are the difficulties that a historian might face when using graphs and statistics?

8 What is biased about this author's choice of graphs? Why might this present a distorted impression of Japanese industrialisation?

## Foreign affairs

After defeating Russia in 1905, Japan continued to pursue an active foreign policy. In 1910, for example, the Japanese extended their influence in East Asia by taking over Korea. At the peace conference

Japanese expansion in the Far East (date of takeover given)

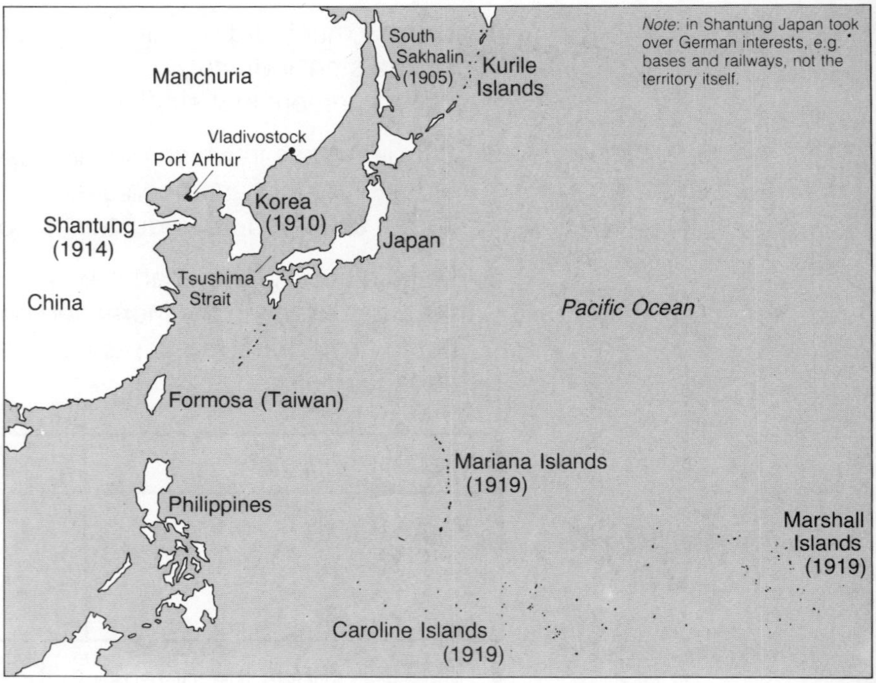


held in 1919 after World War I, Japan was given the right to administer the Mariana, Caroline and Marshall Islands, former German possessions in the South Pacific. Japan's international importance was also recognised when she was given a seat on the Council of the newly created peacekeeping organisation, the League of Nations. In 1921, at the Washington Conference, Japan, Britain, the United States and France agreed to respect each other's interests in the Pacific. Japan also signed a Nine-Power Treaty agreeing to respect the rights of the Chinese. This atmosphere of international co-operation was to continue for the greater part of the 1920s.

## *Hardship and discontent*

Rapid industrial progress brought severe problems for many Japanese people. Because of the movement away from the land in earlier years, between 1917 and 1918 the price of rice, the staple crop, more than doubled and for three weeks in the summer of 1918 disturbances swept the country. These 'rice riots' were bitter and violent. More than one hundred people were killed as police and troops fought running battles with mobs wielding bamboo spears. Rice merchants were beaten or stoned by angry crowds and their property was damaged. As the riots were brought under control, a wave of strikes broke out among workers demanding better pay and improved conditions. The situation was made worse by the sudden collapse in 1921 of the wartime prosperity. This was replaced by a period of economic hardship which affected people from all walks of life.

### *The farmers*

Conditions in the countryside were bleak. Half of Japan's farmers worked on tiny plots of land (less than 1¼ acres), using old-fashioned, inefficient tools and methods. It was a constant struggle to raise enough food for their families to live on. More than 75 per cent of farmers rented their lands from unscrupulous landowners who charged rent in goods, usually half the total rice crop. When times were good the peasants ate millet, barley, sweet potatoes and poor quality rice; when they were bad, they starved.

### *Women in Japan*

One shocking by-product of rural distress can be seen in the appalling treatment of women in 'modern' Japan. In ancient times daughters were frequently sold into prostitution and any 'surplus' female babies were promptly killed in order to prevent them becoming a burden on the family. By the 1920s this barbaric practice had disappeared, but the selling of girls into prostitution still went on. Peasants and poor farmers struggling to survive in the harsh conditions of the countryside often resorted to selling their daughters to the owners of the licensed brothels that were part of all the major Japanese cities. The girls were sold for substantial sums of money and were not allowed to leave until they had worked off their debt. For most girls, this was impossible. According to one estimate it would have taken a girl 189 years to pay back her employers; as a result they were effectively prisoners.

An even more popular practice was to sell females as factory labour. As conditions in the countryside worsened, the owners of silk and cotton mills found themselves guaranteed a constant supply of cheap, undemanding workers. The girls usually lived in the shadow

*Japanese prostitutes on show in a cage in Yokohama. Why do you suppose the women are behind bars?*

of the factories in company dormitories. One observer, John Orchard, described the 'dormitory system' in 1930:

> *Once the girl or woman has been recruited for the factory, she is not allowed to leave the grounds without permission from a company official...permission to leave the factory grounds is difficult to secure and does not come to any one girl more than two or four times a month. ... The young country girls get terribly homesick and many of them run away, but under such close supervision it is not so easy for a girl to break her contract and return to the farm before her year is up. ... An investigation into the physical condition of operatives living in factory dormitories in Tokyo City in May 1930, made by the metropolitan police with the assistance of diet experts, disclosed the fact that a large number of the occupants of factory dormitories are badly undernourished. ... One large factory dormitory, it was said, served miso-shiru (a bean soup) and pickles at breakfast, salted salmon at dinner, and miso-shiru and pickles at supper; and the same menu had been served for years.*
>
> John Orchard: *Japan's Economic Position*, 1930

Not everyone in Japan suffered as a result of modernisation. Great wealth was accumulated by the heads of massive industrial concerns known as zaibatsu, and there were also a rising number of middle-class 'white collar' workers who enjoyed a good standard of living as office clerks, shopkeepers and civil servants. However, the majority of Japanese people experienced great hardship during the 1920s. Some positive measures were taken by the government. In 1925, for example, the Manhood Suffrage Act was passed, giving all males over the age of 25 the right to vote. But such measures did little to help relieve the problems, and the years which followed became increasingly turbulent. Trade unions grew at a steady pace; there were 389 such associations in 1922, rising to 630 by 1929, and with this came an increase in trade disputes. In 1914 there had been just 50 industrial disputes involving almost 8000 workers; by 1929 there were 576, involving more than 77 000 people. Poverty and discontent were common and dangerous features of Japanese society in the 1920s. The people who experienced such difficulties formed a willing audience to the arguments of political extremists who called for decisive and often aggressive action. This would have serious consequences for Japan as it entered the 1930s.

# 2 THE DARK VALLEY

The period 1931–41 in Japanese history has become known as the 'Dark Valley'. During this time the forces of extreme nationalism and the leaders of Japan's armed forces took control of the nation and hurled it headlong down the path of conquest and self-destruction.

Why did so many Japanese people turn their backs on democratic government and give their support to the army generals? One reason was that party politicians frequently failed to act in the interests of the ordinary people. They were more concerned with pleasing the masters of big business or the wealthy landowners from whom they often took bribes. The historian Richard Sims suggests another reason:

> *The Great Depression which had begun in America in 1929 hit the Japanese very hard. Japan's major export was silk. Ironically, though a luxury item, it was produced by peasants who needed the pittance paid for their toil to keep their income above starvation level. When the value of silk exports dropped by two-thirds, many small peasants were ruined, and some families were reduced to selling their daughters into prostitution in order to eat.*
>
> Richard Sims: *Modern Japan*, 1973

The politicians seemed unable to help and the situation was made worse when Japan's trading partners began to place restrictions on cheap Japanese imports.

After 1925, Japan's population increased by about 900 000 a year. For a small country this was a serious problem, since the amount of new land being brought under cultivation was insufficient to feed the extra mouths. Those who tried to escape this situation by emigrating found their way barred by new laws such as the American Immigration Act of 1924. The military solution to these problems was to take over territory in East Asia and to colonise it with Japan's surplus population. The army itself had been greatly influenced by the rise of a number of extreme nationalist associations in the 1920s. By 1930 about 250 such societies existed. Many of them wanted their country to follow a strong foreign policy which would bring additional territory under Japanese control and would result in Japan becoming a powerful nation like Britain or the United States. It was the armed forces which were expected to carry out these plans; they were to overthrow the corrupt and inefficient politicians and to conquer territories on behalf of the Emperor. Such ideas were very popular with the leaders of the army and navy and also among many ordinary Japanese people who looked for an easy way out of their economic difficulties.

## *The attack on Manchuria, 1931*

Japan's first steps along the 'Dark Valley' were taken in China. As a close neighbour of Japan, China was an ideal place for the expansionist plans of the nationalists and army leaders to be tried out. By 1931 Japan already had considerable economic interests in China, especially in the region called Manchuria. Here Japan had stationed more than 10 000 soldiers from her Kwantung Army to protect the Japanese-controlled South Manchurian Railway. However, in the late 1920s, the 'caretaker' role of the army began to be revised in favour of a policy which sought to extend Japan's political control over the region. In 1928, for example, the Japanese assassinated Chang Tso-lin, the Chinese warlord of Manchuria, and tried, unsuccessfully, to assume control of the province.

In 1931 a second attempt brought more positive results. On the night of 18 September an explosion damaged part of the railway track near the town of Mukden. The officers of the Kwantung Army acted swiftly, accusing the Chinese of trying to sabotage Japanese property. The local Chinese garrison was attacked and fighting spread quickly. By March 1932 the whole of Manchuria was under the control of the Japanese army.

Perhaps the most significant aspect of this action was the fact that the army was operating without reference to the government in Tokyo. This was demonstrated quite clearly in the opening weeks of the conflict when the Japanese government agreed to a League of Nations order to withdraw its troops to the South Manchurian Railway zone. The army completely ignored the promises of the politicians and proceeded to stamp its authority on the newly occupied territory. Manchuria was renamed Manchukuo and was declared independent of China. The last of China's Manchu emperors, Pu Yi, was installed as the new head of state, but he was nothing more than a figurehead. The real decisions concerning Manchukuo's future were taken by Japanese army officers. Back in Japan the people were jubilant and a wave of patriotic feeling swept the country. From this point on the politicians found it increasingly difficult to control the armed forces.

---

*Using the evidence: the encouragement of patriotic feeling*

A *Military training was made part of education in 1938 and the time devoted to it, including that spent on indoctrination, increased steadily thereafter, always at the expense of 'unnecessary subjects', that is, those which contributed little to patriotism or practical knowledge. Army officers were attached to schools to supervise this process.*

W.G. Beasley: *The Modern History of Japan*, 1963

B

C

D

E Here are three examples of material used in Japanese schools in the 1930s:

*In reading lessons they [the Japanese children] read the story of Kiguchi Kohei, a trumpeter in the Japanese army during one of the ferocious battles of the Russo-Japanese War, who was found, when the fighting was over, still standing with the trumpet pressed to his lips, but stone dead, a bullet through his heart.*

Tessa Morris-Suzuki: *Showa, an Inside History of Hirohito's Japan*, 1984

*Blossom, blossom, cherry blossom. Here, here, dog, come here. Advance, advance, army advance. The sunrise is bright. Flag of the rising sun, banzai, banzai.*

Opening lines from a primary school reading book, quoted in Tessa Morris-Suzuki's book, as above

*Flag of the rising sun:* the flag of Japan

*I see those faces, hear those voices.*
*My wife and son are waving,*
*Waving their flags until they break.*
*Their message to me is to fight well.*
*I look at the sky, and in the spaces*
*Between the clouds I see them waving still.*
*From the deck of the great fleet of battleships*
*I say goodbye to the land of my birth,*
*Goodbye to my wife and son.*
*I look to the place where the sky arches*
*Above the Imperial Palace*
*And I swear I will fight well.*

Song taught in music lessons, quoted in Tessa Morris-Suzuki's book, as above

F *When he passed through the entertainment district of Ginza [in Tokyo] on his way home from school, Momo sometimes saw earnest-looking women in mompe (the baggy trousers which were to become a sort of national uniform for women during the Pacific War) handing out little cards on the street corners. The women were members of the Patriotic Women's League, and their cards carried warnings which were issued to any woman seen wearing high heels, silk stockings and other unsuitable forms of attire.*

Tessa Morris-Suzuki, as above

G The Japanese authorities used a wide range of techniques to persuade people that their aggressive policies were necessary. The following extract describes what happened to a British journalist arrested in Tokyo in 1940:

*On Monday, July 29, one of the fifteen British prisoners, a Reuters correspondent named Melville Cox, hurtled from an upper-storey window of Tokyo's secret police headquarters and crashed to his death on the pavement below. When attachés from the British Embassy were summoned to pick up his broken body, they counted no less than thirty-five needle punctures in his arms.*

*. . . The Japanese secret police produced a 'suicide note' in Cox's own handwriting which they said he had written before his fall. . . . The note looked as if it had been written with more than one pen, one line at one interrogation, another at the next. Mrs Cox was convinced that it expressed nothing which her husband might have wished to say.*

*. . . The 'suicide note' was advertised in the Japanese press as proof that Britain was spying on Japan and that*

*Englishmen were enemies. The vast majority of Japanese were incensed.*

David Bergamini: *Japan's Imperial Conspiracy*, 1971

1 Suggest one reason why military training was introduced into schools.

2 Why do you think subjects which encouraged patriotism were emphasised in Japanese schools?

3 How do you think the following subjects might have been used to develop patriotic feelings in Japanese schoolchildren:
a) History b) Literature c) Music?

4 As part of their education, Japanese children were taught three important things:
a) The main features of military training.
b) The ways of Japan's ancient samurai warriors.
c) To respect and be loyal to the Emperor.
Examine sources **B**, **C** and **D**. Identify which of the above lessons are being taught to the children in each of the three photographs, then describe how you reached your conclusions.

5 a) Look at source **E**. What theme does each of these examples have in common?
b) Select examples of patriotism from the song.
c) What effect do you think material such as this would have on the way in which Japanese children thought?
d) What do you suppose was the main purpose of using such material?

6 a) Look at source **F**. Explain why the women were objecting to 'silk stockings' and 'high heels'.
b) The Japanese authorities also objected to foreign books, films from Hollywood and modern dancing. What sort of society do you think they wanted to encourage in Japan?

7 a) From source **G**, pick out three details which cast suspicion on the 'suicide' of Melville Cox.
b) What did the Japanese government hope to gain by publicising this incident?
c) Suggest reasons why the Japanese public accepted the story so readily.

8 Why did the Japanese military authorities place great importance on:
a) indoctrination of the young;
b) persuading adults that Western powers were enemies?

## *The China incident*

During the 1930s Japan had advanced unchecked into China (see map). Then, on the night of 7 July 1937, an incident occurred on the Marco Polo bridge in Beijing. Japanese and Chinese troops fired the opening shots in a war between the two nations which was to last for eight savage years.

Following the incident on the Marco Polo bridge, the Japanese mercilessly attacked Chinese troops and civilians. By the end of July Beijing had been captured and in August the great city of Shanghai began to be systematically destroyed. Three months later it was described by a British news correspondent:

> *There is hardly a building standing which has not been gutted by fire. Smouldering ruins and deserted streets present an eerie spectacle, the only living creatures being dogs unnaturally fattened by feasting on corpses.*

Quoted in David Bergamini's book, *Japan's Imperial Conspiracy*, 1971

*Territory taken by Japan in East Asia (date of takeover given)*

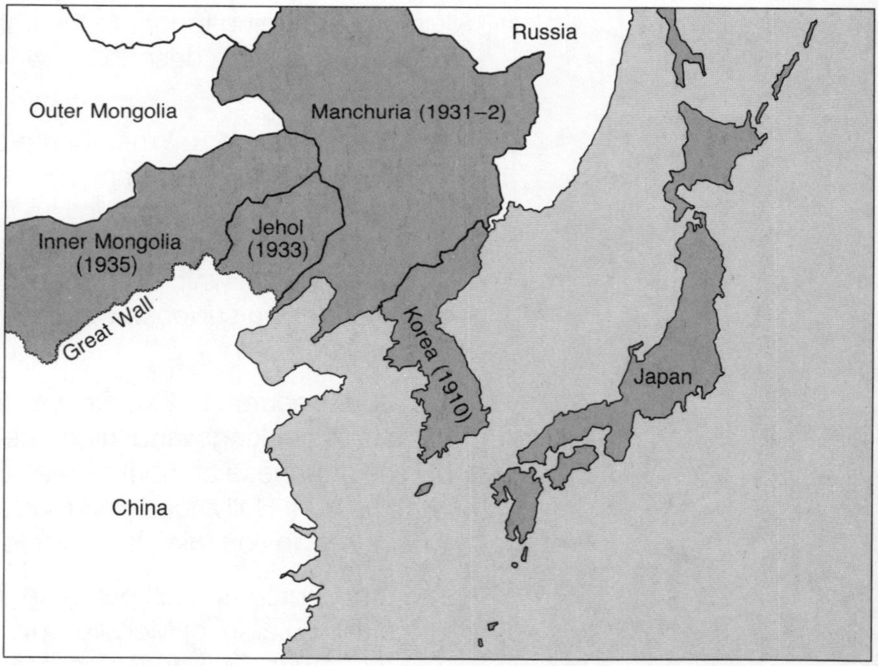


## *The rape of Nanking*

The Japanese now turned their attention to Nanking, the capital of China at this time. The Japanese high command believed that if they captured Nanking, the Chinese would surrender. The city fell on 12 December 1937. During the six weeks that followed, Nanking suffered one of the most brutal and horrific attacks in the history of modern

Japanese soldiers bayoneting Chinese prisoners in Nanking, 1937

warfare. Encouraged by their officers, the Japanese troops went berserk. Thousands of Chinese prisoners of war were butchered in the first few days. They were used as live targets for bayonet practice or to test the efficiency of machine guns. Some were burned to death, others were beheaded. Still more were buried up to their necks in the earth and died under the hooves of horses or the wheels of tanks. This orgy of violence soon extended to the civilian population. Whole areas of the city were set alight by Japanese arson squads, but not before they had been looted and all valuable property had been moved to army depots. On 15 December lorry loads of Chinese women and girls were taken from refugee camps within the city and moved to Japanese army barracks. Here they were raped, sometimes up to 20 times a night, by off-duty soldiers. Some of the victims were less than 12 years old.

Nanking's nightmare ended in January 1938. By that time one-third of the city had been burned to the ground and some 200 000 people had been murdered; in addition around 20 000 women had been raped. The agonies suffered by the people of Nanking did not move China's leaders to surrender as the Japanese had hoped. Instead their resistance hardened and the war continued at the cost of over two million lives until the defeat of Japan in 1945.

---

*Questions*

1 At the time of the Nanking atrocities the Japanese claimed that the women had not been raped but were prostitutes who had fled when the soldiers had arrived in the city. The Japanese maintained that they had simply returned the women to resume their 'business'. What is your opinion of this explanation?

2 The Japanese authorities would not allow news of the Nanking outrages to reach the Japanese people. Why do you think this measure was taken?

---

## *The road to war*

The ambitions and actions of Japan's military leaders began to cause grave concern among Western powers as the 1930s progressed. The money spent on Japan's armed forces increased dramatically from 500 million yen (30 per cent of the total government budget) in 1931, to 4000 million yen (70 per cent of the total government budget) in 1937–8.

Plans began to take shape to turn the whole of East Asia into a Japanese-dominated economic unit to be called 'The Greater East Asia Co-Prosperity Sphere'. This would ultimately mean taking over

Western interests in such places as Malaya, Singapore and the Dutch East Indies. In the attack on China in 1937, people from the West had been killed and their property destroyed. The Japanese had even attacked British and American naval vessels operating on the Yangtze River; the sinking of the USS *Panay* in December 1937 provoked a storm of anger in the United States.

In spite of these actions, Japan's expansionist plans went ahead with little more than verbal protests from the West. However, as the war against China dragged on, this was to change. In 1940, in an effort to cut China off from its supply routes, Japan occupied Indo-China. The United States, Britain and Holland responded by refusing to send strategic supplies to Japan. This included a ban on the export of oil. For Japan this was a very disturbing move. With less than two years' worth of oil reserves, Japan faced the prospect of a humiliating defeat if stocks could not be replenished. The military authorities knew that if Japan's gains of the previous ten years were to be kept, and if the dream of creating an empire in East Asia was to become a reality, they would have to take on and defeat the Western powers, in particular the United States of America. In a decision that was to change the course of Japan's history, the generals and admirals began preparations for an all-out war. On the morning of 7 December 1941, the Japanese air force attacked part of the American Pacific Fleet at anchor in the Hawaiian naval base of Pearl Harbor. The following day the United States declared war on Japan.

*The end of USS* California, *Pearl Harbor, 1941*

# 3 THE OCCUPATION

On 15 August 1945 Emperor Hirohito announced the surrender of Japan. The dream of creating an empire in East Asia was shattered and the disastrous rule of the generals was over. In the final year of the conflict the horrors and hardships of war were brought home to the Japanese people. Food was very difficult to find and people began to starve. On 1 November 1944, American B29 aircraft began their fire-bombing raids on the Japanese mainland. Japan's wooden cities were consumed in terrifying fire storms and by the time of the surrender 668 000 people had perished in them. Fusako Sasaki was a teenager when the raids hit Tokyo. She recalls the scene of horror after the bombers had returned to base:

> *Stacked up corpses were being hauled away on lorries. Everywhere there was the stench of the dead and of smoke. I saw places on the pavement where people had been roasted to death. At last I comprehended first hand what an air raid meant.*
>
> Quoted in *Purnell's History of the Second World War*, 1974

In August 1945, Hiroshima and Nagasaki were obliterated by the awesome power of the newly developed atomic bomb. In the same month the Soviet Union declared war on Japan and began to advance from the north. Emperor Hirohito's decision to surrender saved Japan from almost certain destruction and marked the beginning of the American occupation of his defeated and exhausted country.

---

### *Using the evidence: Japan in defeat*

In charge of the occupation was General Douglas MacArthur, the Supreme Commander for the Allied Powers, more commonly known as SCAP. When he arrived in Japan he found the country in a terrible condition. The Japanese, who had never before been defeated in war, were confused and frightened, and they expected the worst of the occupying forces.

A *The government made a lot of propaganda in those last few months about what would happen if the Americans came—how they would make us into slaves, and all the women would be raped.*

Saito Mutsuo, quoted in Tessa Morris-Suzuki's book, *Showa, an Inside History of Hirohito's Japan*, 1984

B *We had heard the rumours that the occupation forces would rape all Japanese women, and Mother said to us: 'When we get back, we must cut our hair short, and make our faces black with charcoal. That way we may possibly be safe.'*

Tsutsumi Ayako, quoted in Tessa Morris-Suzuki's book, as above

C *Later that day [15 August 1945, the day of the Japanese surrender] one of the lads in the squad—he'd been a volunteer who'd gone straight from school to military cadet college—he took a machine gun and pointed the barrel into his mouth, and he put his foot on the trigger and fired.*

Saito Mutsuo, as above

D *The destruction of Tokyo, 1945*

E *Victor and vanquished: General MacArthur receives Emperor Hirohito at the American Embassy in Tokyo*

1 What did many Japanese people fear would happen to them when the Americans began to occupy their country?

2 How is the spread of these fears explained in sources A and B? How reliable would such information have been?

3 Suggest reasons why the soldier in source C committed suicide after learning of Japan's surrender.

4 Study source D, which shows what central Tokyo was like in 1945. Make a list of all the problems the Japanese people would have faced trying to live in such conditions.

5 Look at source E. The Japanese government tried to prevent people from seeing this photograph. Can you suggest why they wanted to ban its publication?

## *The occupation begins*

The Japanese people faced many difficulties such as food shortages, disease and unemployment during the first months of the occupation. However, they were at least spared the problems of dealing with a vengeful occupying army. MacArthur ordered his troops to behave responsibly at all times, and for the most part they obeyed. As the occupation progressed, many Western ways began to be adopted once again by the Japanese. The chewing of gum became popular. Women gave up wearing traditional clothes in favour of American-style skirts and stockings. Men, too, began to wear American casual clothes, and baseball became a nationwide passion.

> *These were the days when it was the most fashionable thing in the world to be seen about town carrying a copy of* Reader's Digest *and it was pleasing to be able to stroll around the Tokyo streets in American slacks and an American sweater, lighting Lucky Strike cigarettes with a Zip pocket lighter.*
>
> Tessa Morris-Suzuki: *Showa, an Inside History of Hirohito's Japan*, 1984

*Japanese children eager to learn a new American ball game*

The first aim of the occupation was to make sure that Japan could never again threaten the peace of the world. Accordingly, over five million troops were demobilised and military installations and supplies were destroyed. Japan was also punished for her aggressive behaviour. All territory which had been gained since 1868 was taken away from Japanese possession. Thousands of war criminals were put on trial and more than 900 of them were executed. In addition, about 200 000 people believed to have supported Japan's pre-war military government were removed from their positions of responsibility. This 'purge' was directed at key figures in such areas as education, politics, administration, business, the press and radio.

These measures were quickly followed by a series of reforms designed to turn Japan into a democratic and responsible nation.

*Japanese wartime leaders stand trial as war criminals*

## *The constitution*

In the first year of the occupation perhaps the most important action taken by SCAP was to prepare a new constitution for Japan. At first, the Japanese were allowed to produce their own suggestions. However, these proved unacceptable to the Americans who then drew up their own proposals and forced them on the Japanese government. The new constitution came into force in October 1946. It gave Japan a system which was similar in many ways to those of the United States and Britain. The diagram below shows its main features.

*The new constitution*

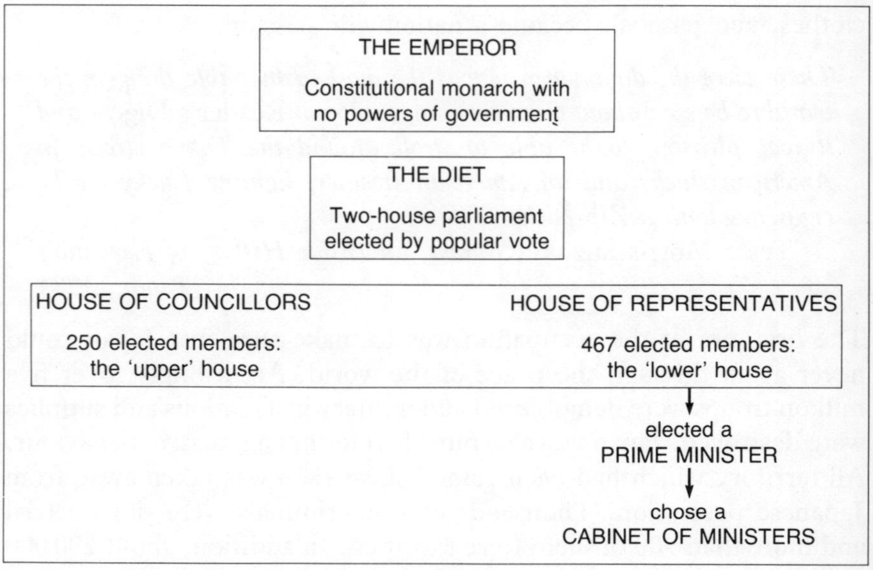


***The new constitution and the Emperor***

The 1946 constitution changed the status of the Emperor of Japan. Prior to this time he was regarded by the Japanese as a divine being, a descendant of the gods. He was rarely seen by the people, but his image was the object of daily worship throughout Japan. The constitution formalised the decision taken by the Emperor in January 1946 to give up his divine status. Although he retained his title, he no longer had any power and was to be regarded simply as a man who owed his position to the will of the people.

***The new constitution and the position of women***

In the election of April 1946 more than 13 million women voted for the first time and 38 women were elected to parliament. This important development was the direct result of Article 14 of the new constitution which stated:

> *All of the people are equal under the law and there shall be no discrimination in political, economic or social relations because of race, creed, sex, social status or family origin.*

General MacArthur later noted that this had a significant effect on the status of Japanese women:

> *The Japanese women were quick to take advantage of this new status under the constitution. They found jobs in professions where they had never been before. In the next five years some 2000 of them became policewomen. They took an active part in the various labour unions, a million and a half of them joining workmen's organizations. For the first time in Japanese history they fought for and secured laws giving them the same pay and same hours as men. They even asked for and received maternity leave.*
>
> Douglas MacArthur: *Reminiscences*, 1964

*Japanese women voting for the first time in the elections of April 1946*

***The new constitution and the no-war clause***

Article 9 of the constitution was very important. It stated:

> *... the Japanese people forever renounce war as a sovereign right of the nation and the threat or use of force as means of settling international disputes.*

This part of the constitution was extremely popular in Japan. Having recently suffered the horrors of war, the Japanese were only too pleased to turn their backs on the use of military force as a solution to their problems.

---

*Questions*

1 In what ways was the constitution given to Japan similar to the system of government in Britain?

2 Suggest one reason why the Japanese might have been unhappy with this constitution.

3 How did the constitution change the status of the Emperor?

4 MacArthur claimed that the constitution had an enormous impact on the position of women in Japanese society. How reliable do you think his assessment of their status is? What problems might Japanese women have faced despite the constitution?

5 Why do you think the Americans were keen to include Article 9 in the constitution?

---

Having reformed the constitution, MacArthur set about changing other areas of Japanese life.

| *Area of reform* | *Changes made* |
|---|---|
| The land | The aim was to increase the number of people who owned the land they farmed. Five million acres were distributed among three million tenants at affordable prices. By 1950, 90 per cent of Japan's agricultural land was in the hands of private owners. |
| Trade unions | The weak prewar trade unions were strengthened by the Trade Union Act of 1945 and the Labour Relations Act of 1946. All Japanese workers now had the right to form unions and to strike. Union membership increased from 5300 in 1945 to seven million in 1948. In 1947 a Labour Standards Act guaranteed better working conditions and introduced health insurance and compensation for accidents at work. |
| The zaibatsu | Great industrial combines called zaibatsu dominated the economy of Japan in the years before World War II. MacArthur wanted to break up these powerful organisations and began to do so in 1947. |
| Education | Compulsory education was extended from six to nine years' duration. Higher education was encouraged and state control of education was considerably reduced. |

---

## *Using the evidence: a change in policy*

By the end of 1947 Japan had been punished, demilitarised and transformed through a series of reforms. Some observers, including MacArthur himself, were suggesting that it was now time for the United States to end the occupation. Instead, the opening months of 1948 saw not an end to SCAP's activities, but a change in their direction. This change in policy was caused by the situation in Japan and in the world outside.

A *In the first place, American authorities encouraged the growth of the self-defence forces of Japan, in police reserves and in land, sea and air arms, in spite of Article 9 of the constitution renouncing war. Action against the zaibatsu was abandoned and the dismantling of plants ceased.*

W. Scott Morton: *Japan, its History and its Culture*, 1970

B *Washington had come to the conclusion that an economic revival of Japan would be in the interest of the United States; consequently, America embarked on a programme of rehabilitating Japan's trade and industries.*

Baron E.J. Lewe Van Advard: *Japan from Surrender to Peace*, 1953

C *Then came the revision of the Trade Union Act in 1949, putting restrictions on the political activity of many workers . . . over 20,000 [Communists] were said to have been dismissed from jobs in government, education and industry during 1949 and 1950, some even from the unions themselves. It was also in 1949 that MacArthur authorized the Japanese government to review the application of the purges of 1946 and 1947. Progress was slow at first, but the pace quickened after June 1950, so that almost all those originally affected had regained their political rights by 1951.*

W.G. Beasley: *The Modern History of Japan*, 1963

D

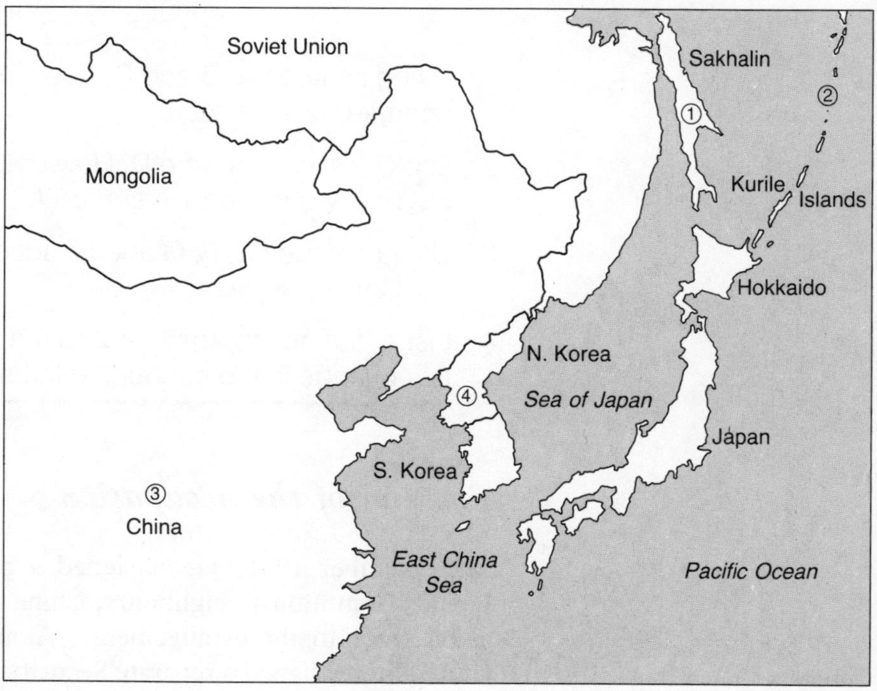


① Sakhalin given to Russia by Japan

② Kurile Islands given to Russia by Japan

③ China fell to the Communists in 1949

④ Communist North Korea invaded South Korea. The war lasted from 1950 to 1953

E *In 1948, the occupation was costing the United States about 450 million dollars a year.*

David John Lu: *Sources of Japanese History*, volume 2, 1974

F *Let's not kid ourselves. We need a strong Japan, for one of these days we'll have to face Russia, and we'll need an ally. Japan is it.*

Major Ben Locke, quoted in Mark Gayn's book, *Japan Diary*, 1948

G *The men who were most active in building up and running Japan's war machine were often the ablest and most successful business leaders of that country and their services would in many instances contribute to the economic recovery of Japan.*

Extract from a speech by Kenneth C. Royall, Secretary of the US Army, 1948

H *We had trouble with the Communists in the labour movement. They obtained control of some of the unions and eventually called a general strike. It was a very difficult situation for me. I did not want to stand in the way of newly organized labourers attempting to assert their rights, but I was not going to let a few Communist leaders use the strike as a political weapon and in so doing wreck the whole economy.*

Douglas MacArthur: *Reminiscences*, 1964

1 Using sources **A**, **B** and **C**, describe how SCAP's policies changed after 1948.

2 Look closely at source **D**. How does this map help to explain the policy described in source **A**?

3 Using sources **E**, **F**, **G** and **H**, account for the other changes in SCAP's policies.

4 List a) the advantages, and b) the disadvantages to Japan of this change in the conduct of the occupation.

## *The end of the occupation*

In September 1951, Japan signed a peace treaty with 48 nations. Japan's Communist neighbours, China and the Soviet Union, refused to be party to the arrangements. Along with the peace treaty, the United States signed a separate Security Pact with Japan. This allowed

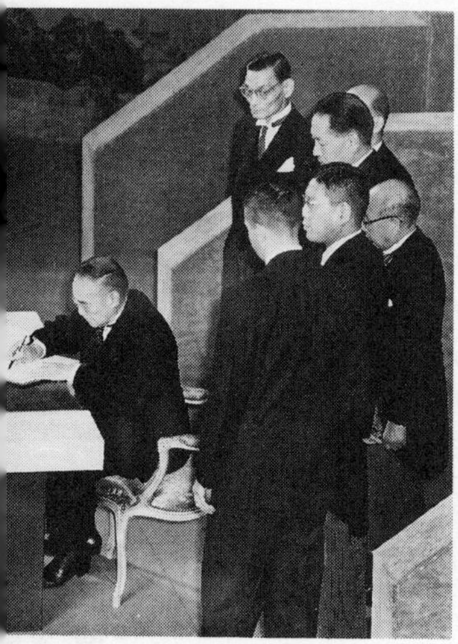

*The end of the occupation. Shigeru Yoshida signing the peace treaty in San Francisco, 1951*

US military forces to be stationed in and around Japan to help maintain peace in the Far East and to protect Japan against armed attack. The San Francisco peace and security arrangements came into force on 28 April 1952. The occupation was officially ended and Japan once more became an independent nation.

---

### *Using the evidence: opinion poll*

Shortly after the San Francisco treaty came into effect, the Asahi newspaper carried out a survey to discover what the Japanese people felt about the peace treaty and the occupation. The following questions and answers are taken from the survey.

1 *Do you think that as a result of the coming into effect of the peace treaty, Japan is now independent? Or do you think Japan is not independent?*
*Became independent* .......... *41%*
*Independent in name only* .......... *32%*
*Not independent* .......... *8%*
*No opinion* .......... *19%*

2 *Do you think Japan should conclude a peace treaty with the Soviet Union, or in your opinion such a treaty need not be concluded?*
*In favour of peace treaty* .......... *54%*
*Not in favour of peace treaty* .......... *20%*
*No opinion* .......... *26%*

3 *Do you think relations between Japan and Communist China can remain as they are, or cannot remain the way they are?*
*Can remain the way they are* .......... *11%*
*Cannot remain the way they are* .......... *57%*
*No opinion* .......... *32%*

4 *During the period when Japan was under occupation, was there anything which the SCAP or the Japanese government did, which in your opinion was good?*
*Yes* .......... *47%*
*No* .......... *14%*
*No opinion* .......... *39%*

5 *Was there anything they did which you consider to be undesirable?*
*Yes* .......... *28%*
*No* .......... *26%*
*No opinion* .......... *46%*

6 *US troops continue to remain on Japanese soil, even after the conclusion of the occupation. Why are they in Japan?*

| | |
|---|---|
| *To protect Japan* | *21%* |
| *To guard against aggression by the Soviet Union and Communist China and Communist forces* | *18%* |
| *To maintain Japan's internal security* | *13%* |
| *Due to Japan's lack of defence power* | *11%* |
| *For the protection of the US herself* | *4%* |
| *To place Japan under surveillance* | *3%* |
| *No opinion* | *30%* |

7 *Do you wish to see US troops remain in Japan?*

| | |
|---|---|
| *Yes, hope they remain* | *48%* |
| *No, hope they do not* | *20%* |
| *We have no choice, either way is fine* | *16%* |
| *No opinion* | *16%* |

Survey reprinted in David John Lu's book, *Sources of Japanese History*, volume 2, 1974

1 What percentage of those questioned felt that after 1952 Japan was not really an independent country? Why might these people hold this opinion?

2 Why were so many people in favour of a peace treaty with the Soviet Union and better relations with China? Suggest one reason why some Japanese people still wanted to resist such developments.

3 How do you think the following people might have answered questions 4 and 5:
a) a Japanese farmer who rented land before 1945;
b) a Japanese woman;
c) a Japanese Communist?
Give reasons for your answer.

4 If a sample of the public in a) the United States, and b) the Soviet Union had been asked question 6, what answer do you think would have been the most popular in each case?

5 Given the answers to question 7, would it be accurate to say that the Japanese people were entirely happy with the continued presence of US troops in Japan?

6 The information in this opinion poll was gathered by interviewing 2523 people throughout Japan. Do you think this is likely to give an accurate picture of Japanese public opinion as a whole? What problems are there in using this type of evidence?

# 4 FOREIGN RELATIONS

## *Peace and stability*

Japan's behaviour in the 1930s and during the years of the Pacific War had caused considerable resentment and suspicion among her neighbours. This continued even after the signing of the San Francisco Peace Treaty. Australia and New Zealand, for example, pushed hard for a Security Treaty (ANZUS pact) with the United States, which gave them American guarantees of protection against aggression in the Pacific. A similar agreement was made between the United States and the Philippines. Some countries, including Indonesia, Communist China, India and the Soviet Union, refused to sign the peace treaty with Japan. This was an indication of the continued ill-feeling against her.

During the 1950s and '60s, Japan worked hard to restore friendly relations with her former enemies. In October 1956 the Japanese Prime Minister, Ichiro Hatoyama, visited Moscow and signed an agreement which re-opened diplomatic relations between Japan and the Soviet Union. Arrangements were made to make compensation payments to Burma (1954), the Philippines (1956) and Indonesia (1958), countries which Japan had invaded during World War II. In 1956 Japan was admitted to the United Nations and eight years later joined the Organization for Economic Co-operation and Development (OECD). A peace treaty with South Korea, Japan's closest neighbour, was signed in 1965. This restored normal relations and gave valuable economic assistance to Korea. Japan was keen to give aid to other South-East Asian countries. She was, for example, the biggest contributor to the Asian Development Bank set up in Manila in 1966.

Below: *the 1964 Tokyo Olympic Games symbolised Japan's return to international respectability*

Below right: *the Shinkansen 'bullet' train, part of Japan's new image on show to the world in 1964*

## *Relations with China*

In December 1951 the Japanese Prime Minister, Shigeru Yoshida, wrote in a letter to the US government:

> *I can assure you that the Japanese government has no intention to conclude a bilateral treaty with the Communist regime of China.*

*bilateral treaty:* an arrangement made between two countries

Shigeru Yoshida was very worried by the recent Communist takeover in China. He claimed that a treaty of friendship and alliance agreed between China and the Soviet Union in 1950 was aimed against Japan, and he suspected that the Chinese Communists were giving assistance to the Japanese Communist Party. Therefore, when in April 1952 Japan signed a peace treaty with China, it was not with Mao Zedong's Communists on mainland China, but with the island of Taiwan (also called Formosa), home of the Chinese Nationalists who had been forced to leave China when the Communists took over in 1949. This arrangement suited the US government, which opposed the Chinese Communists and recognised Taiwan as the official voice of China. During the 1960s trade between Japan and Communist China expanded slowly, but diplomatic relations remained poor. The situation was not helped in 1964 when China, carrying out her first nuclear test, exploded an atomic bomb at Lob Nor; after Hiroshima and Nagasaki the Japanese were particularly nervous about the spread of nuclear weapons. During the same period, relations between China and the Soviet Union turned sour and China began to look elsewhere for friendship. As a result, in 1971, US President Richard Nixon announced his intention to visit Beijing. Japan was quick to follow and in 1972 Prime Minister Kakuei Tanaka flew to China and restored normal relations between the two countries. In 1978 a treaty of peace and friendship was signed.

*Prime Minister Kakuei Tanaka meets the Chinese leader Mao Zedong in Beijing, 1972*

*Questions*

1 How would the following have helped Japan to re-establish itself in world affairs after 1952?
   a) The 'peace' constitution and refusal to build up the armed forces.
   b) Admission to the United Nations.
   c) The giving of overseas aid.
   d) Restoring diplomatic relations and signing treaties of peace and friendship.

2 Why do you think Japan waited until 1972 before restoring normal relations with Communist China?

## *Japan and the United States*

> *Historically, whenever Japan took a path counter to the United States, the country suffered; and whenever the two worked closely together, Japan prospered.*
>
> Eisaku Sato, Japanese Prime Minister, 1964–72

Since the ending of the occupation in 1952, Japan and the United States have maintained friendly relations. Both countries have benefited and Japan has certainly prospered. Trade between Japan and the US is an important part of both nations' economies. The Security Pact offers Japan the protection of America's armed forces, while large numbers of US military bases are maintained on Japanese soil. These bases are vital to the defence of American interests in the Pacific. However, the relationship is far from perfect. In the years after 1952 a number of incidents occurred which placed great strain on relations between the two countries. Soon after the peace treaty was signed, Communist-led riots broke out in Tokyo. American cars were overturned and burned. The protesters complained bitterly that in spite of the ending of the occupation, there were still 2824 US military bases in Japan, in which 260 000 American troops were stationed. In 1952 the ban on reporting incidents of bad behaviour by the occupying troops was lifted. The Japanese press did not hesitate to print any story which showed the American soldier in a bad light, be it a serious crime such as rape, or the rather peculiar practice of throwing Japanese citizens into the Imperial Palace moat in Tokyo.

In 1960, when the Security Pact came up for renewal, there were serious protest riots in Tokyo. Disturbances occurred within the Japanese parliament when the police removed politicians opposed to the treaty. In the face of these problems, US President Dwight D. Eisenhower was forced to cancel a planned visit to Japan. America's

Riots in Tokyo, May Day 1952

reluctance to return the island of Okinawa to Japan also caused resentment, especially as it was used as a base for US bombers during the war with Vietnam in the 1960s.

---

*Question*

During the occupation of Japan, General MacArthur claimed that the troops under his command behaved extremely well. Is there anything in what you have just read to suggest that this claim could have been exaggerated?

---

*Using the evidence: the Lucky Dragon*

Historians are often faced with the problems of gaps and contradictions in the evidence they use, making it difficult for them to produce an accurate picture of past events. You can see some of these problems in the evidence below, which concerns another incident that strained relations between Japan and the United States, in 1954.

A *Japanese newspapers are publishing reports that twenty-three Japanese fishermen on board the fishing craft Fukurya Maru (Lucky Dragon) were physically affected by the atomic explosion organized by the United States at Bikini in the Marshall Islands, on March 1st. According to these reports the Fukurya Maru was fishing some 80 miles west of Bikini when, at 3 a.m. the fishermen saw a flash, followed by a mushroom-shaped cloud, and seven minutes later felt the force of an explosion. Two men were on deck at the time, and they were later said to be most affected. The explosion was said to be followed about an hour and a half later by a shower of ash, which continued to fall for about two hours. The fishermen paid no heed to these events until three days later, when they began to develop blisters. The ship then quickly returned to its home port of Yaizu, 30 miles south-west of Tokyo, where the two men who had been on deck at the time of the explosion were taken to hospital and later transferred to Tokyo with symptoms of falling hair, blisters on the face and watering eyes. The other men are reported to have been affected in less degree. The matter was raised in the Japanese Diet today by left-wing Socialist members, and Mr Okazaki, the Foreign Minister, told the House that the United States had warned Japan that the danger zone during the atomic tests at Bikini extended 200 nautical miles east and west of the island and 150 nautical miles north and south.*

*The Times*, 17 March 1954

B Crew members' accounts of the Bikini incident:

*Midway:* American naval base

*If we had realized how sick we were, we would have put into Midway and asked the Americans there for help, but we did not know.*

*I felt much warmer than usual, almost as if I was glowing, and several others remarked that they felt the same way. Again we paid little attention to this because we were so used to sunburn and windburn.*

*Pikadon:* the Japanese word for atomic bomb

*We were very depressed and some of the crew grumbled 'Pikadon', but others said it could not be. I think someone said it was probably the dust from some volcanic explosion.*

*Life* magazine, 25 March 1954

C *Mr Strauss [Chairman of the American Atomic Energy Commission, which was involved with the Bikini test] said that the only fish affected were those in the Fukurya Maru and American inspectors had found no instance of radioactivity in any shipment of fish from Pacific waters.*

*The Times*, 1 April 1954

*geiger counter:* device used for measuring radioactivity

D *A Tokyo University research team today confirmed that two more fishing boats had been contaminated by the March 1st hydrogen bomb explosion, and that three others showed 'strong geiger counter reaction'. The three 'suspects' had been operating about 1000 miles from the Bikini bomb site. The two contaminated boats were within 800 miles. The crews of both boats have been sent to hospital and their fish hauls have been dumped by government order.*

Reuters, printed in *The Times*, 1 April 1954

E *In the end it became known that the fall-out from the Bikini bomb had been on a scale and in a direction not expected by the scientists who had planned the operation; and it was admitted that the fishing boat had been outside the danger zone.*

Richard Storry: *A History of Modern Japan*, 1960

1 The Chairman of the American Atomic Energy Commission, Mr Strauss, claimed at the time of this incident that adequate warning had been given about the dangers of being near Bikini when the test was taking place. Do the crew members' accounts suggest that they were unaware of any test being carried out? Give reasons for your answer.

2 a) Sources **C** and **D** appeared in the same newspaper on the same day. What explanations could you offer for the inconsistency of these reports?

b) As a historian, what additional information would you need in order to decide which of these reports was the most accurate?

c) If one of these reports was written using false information, would it be of no use to the historian?

3 At the time of the incident many Japanese people believed that the *Lucky Dragon* had been fishing outside the official danger zone. How does source **D** help to support this claim?

4 Source **E** was written in 1960. Why might this source give a more accurate account of the incident than the others?

---

## *The 'Nixon shocks'*

In 1971 Japan experienced the so-called 'Nixon shocks'. US President Richard Nixon announced that he intended to visit Communist China to establish relations between China and the United States. The Japanese were astonished. For years they had followed the American policy of hostility to the Communists and had as a result denied themselves access to a potentially enormous trading market. Now they were not even consulted about the intended visit and Japanese pride was dealt a serious blow. The second 'shock' was a 10 per cent surcharge placed on goods coming into the United States, in an effort to curb imports. Since Japanese products made up a large part of America's imports, the measure hit Japanese industry particularly hard.

B *Japan celebrates the American bicentennial: one of several Statues of Liberty set up in Tokyo in 1976*

Although there have been problems, Japan and the United States have continued to work together as friends and allies. The partnership was strengthened in 1972, when America returned the island of Okinawa to Japanese control.

---

*Using the evidence: how Japan and the United States view each other*

A *. . . the most important bilateral relationship in the world, bar none!*

Ambassador Mike Mansfield on the US–Japan partnership, quoted in Roger Buckley's book, *Japan Today*, 1985

C *. . . Our relationship with the United States is of vital importance to the security and prosperity of Japan. It constitutes the very basis of our foreign policy.*

Japanese Foreign Minister Yoshimasa Ohira, in a speech to the Diet, 23 January 1963

D *I will tell you one thing, get it into your head right now; [with regard to defence] if there is any country getting by without paying their share, it is Japan.*

L. Mendel Rivers, Chairman of the American Armed Services Committee, quoted in *The Japan Reader*, volume 2, 1973

E *. . . the present Mutual Security Treaty is perceived by many Japanese as a kind of continuation of the American occupation.*

Kinhide Mushakoji: *Japan Institute of Foreign Affairs*, 1969–70

F *In the March 1968 survey by Joji Watanuki and others, 55.2% thought that 'the Treaty [Mutual Security Pact] endangers Japan's safety', while 21.2% felt that it 'contributes to Japan's safety'.*

Quoted in the *Japan Institute of Foreign Affairs*, 1965–68

G *According to a poll conducted by the Gallup organization in September 1968 [in America], Japan was ranked 17th among 30 nations in terms of trustworthiness.*

Quoted in the *Japan Institute of Foreign Affairs*, 1969–70

1 Ambassador Mike Mansfield and Foreign Minister Yoshimasa Ohira both speak on behalf of their governments. What is the 'official' view on the Japan–US relationship?

2 How does the official view differ from the findings of the public opinion surveys in sources F and G?

3 Suggest ways in which some Japanese people think their safety might be at risk because of the Security Pact with the United States.

4 What criticisms are contained in sources D and E?

5 State which source or sources quoted above you would use to support the following statements:
   a) The Japanese government is keen to encourage good relations with the United States.
   b) Many Japanese people would prefer their country to be neutral in world affairs.
   c) Some Americans are suspicious of the Japanese because they grow rich while sheltering under the American defence umbrella.

6 Relations between Japan and the United States have sometimes been difficult. Suggest reasons why, in spite of these problems, the Japan–US partnership has lasted since 1952.

---

## *Japan's relationship with the rest of the world*

It has sometimes been said that Japan's foreign policy consists of nothing more than using the rest of the world as one great market in which it can sell its goods. It has been claimed that Japan prefers to remain out of international affairs. Certainly Japan is cautious when dealing with other countries; the Japanese remind themselves every year in moving ceremonies at Hiroshima and Nagasaki about the dangers of an aggressive foreign policy. Japan reacts to international events with great care. In 1983, for example, a Korean airliner was shot down by Soviet fighters and Japanese citizens were among those who died. The Japanese government could not decide what to do at first, but eventually 'punished' the Russians by refusing to allow civil servants to fly with the Soviet national airline, Aeroflot.

However, the Japanese have been known to respond swiftly to events when national interests are at stake. On 6 October 1973 war broke out between Israel and Egypt and other Arab nations. The prospect of Japan's Middle Eastern oil supplies being reduced to a trickle caused panic. Against the advice of the United States and other Western countries, Japan declared a pro-Arab policy. Envoys were sent to visit nine Arab nations and Israel was criticised by the Japanese government. The Arab countries soon declared Japan to be a 'friendly country' and the oil began to flow to Japan once more.

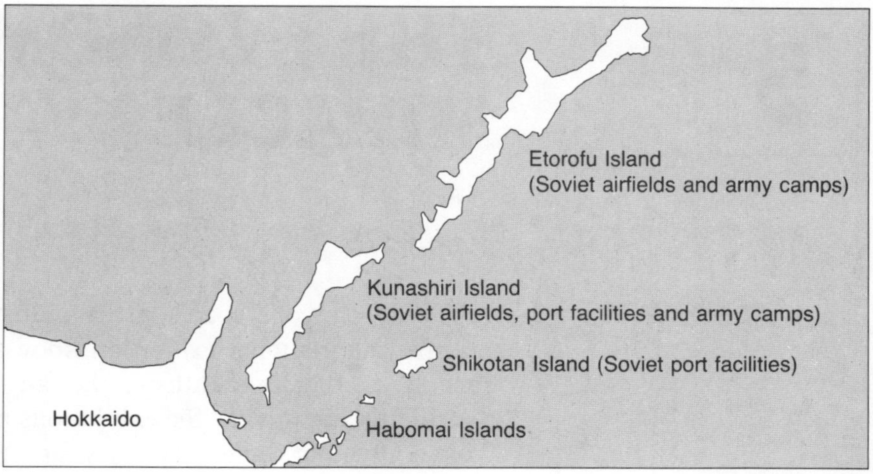


*The disputed northern islands. Why do you think the Japanese are so concerned about Russia's occupation of these islands?*

Japan's worst record in foreign affairs has been with the Soviet Union. Although diplomatic relations were restored in 1956, a peace treaty has never been signed between the two countries. The main dispute is over the islands which lie to the north of Japan (see map). These islands have been occupied by the Soviets since 1945 and Japan would very much like to see them returned. Japan has been a constant critic of Soviet actions, opposing the invasion of Afghanistan in 1979 and the threat to move SS20 missiles from Eastern Europe to the Soviet border with Asia.

Japan may not have a very active foreign policy; it does not even provide troops for United Nations peacekeeping missions, for example. But it is without doubt a very important world power. In 1979 Japan hosted the fifth summit conference of leading industrial nations, the first such conference to be held outside the West. Japan's importance can also be seen in the willingness of world leaders to go there for meetings and discussions. In 1983, for example, Prime Minister Nakasone welcomed the West German Chancellor, the Secretary General of the Chinese Communist Party and the President of the United States to his country, an indication of the attention and respect commanded by Japan in the modern world.

*Prime Minister Nakasone (third from the right) at the 1984 London summit*

# 5 THE ECONOMIC MIRACLE

## *Expo '70*

In 1970, one of Japan's great industrial cities, Osaka, staged a massive international exhibition known as Expo '70. It was a huge success. In the six months of the fair, 64 million people visited the Senri Hills site to view the exhibitions put on by 77 nations. Like the Tokyo Olympic Games six years earlier, Expo '70 was in many ways symbolic. It represented the staggering economic and technological progress made by Japan just 25 years after the devastation of World War II. In 1945, 44 per cent of all Japan's factories had been destroyed and the transport system was in chaos. Production had dropped by 75 per cent since before the war and the people faced the misery of unemployment, hunger and homelessness. In addition there was the problem of raw materials; Japan has virtually none of her own and has to import around 97 per cent of the iron ore and 99 per cent of the oil needed by heavy industry. In the aftermath of the war Japan could find neither the money to pay for such goods nor countries willing to supply them. The situation was bleak indeed.

By the time the Osaka exposition opened, however, Japan had become the third largest economic power, her performance being bettered only by the 'superpowers', the Soviet Union and the United States. The products of Japanese industry were, by this time, familiar throughout the world. Cars, motorcycles, cameras, televisions and video recorders all proudly bore the label 'Made in Japan', and the names of Japan's big manufacturers such as Toyota, Honda, Hitachi, Sony and Toshiba had become well known to consumers everywhere.

## *Industrial superpower*

Japan's astonishing economic expansion began in the immediate postwar period with the 'priority production system'. This geared the economy towards building up the basic industries such as steel and coal. As output in these industries began to expand, a firm base was laid upon which the rest of the economy could build. Through the 1950s and '60s the economy took off and advanced at a bewildering pace. Between 1960 and 1970 the annual growth rate in Japan was about 11 per cent. This was a figure which other industrialised nations could only dream about; the United States, for example, could only manage a rate of just over 4 per cent, and this under normal circumstances would have been considered a very good performance. By

*Percentages of world output being produced by Japan*

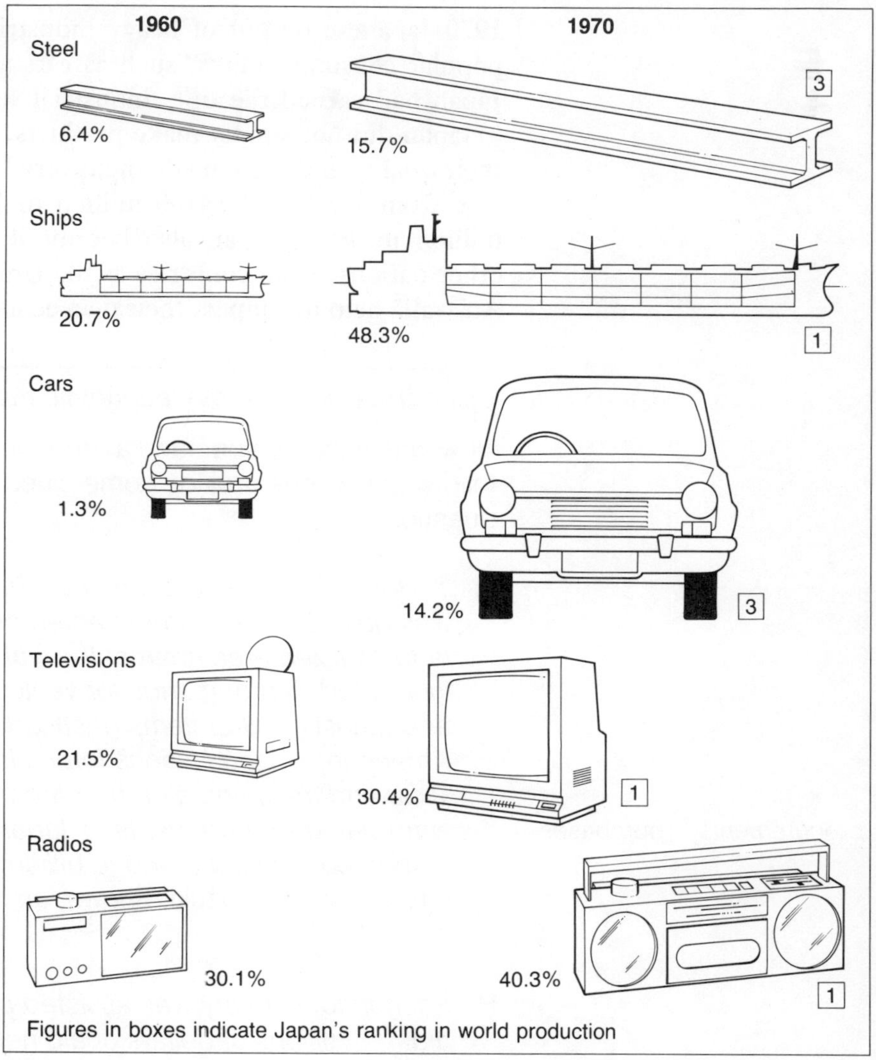


*Giant oil tanker under construction at Yokohama*

1970 Japanese output of heavy industrial goods, such as steel, and popular consumer items, such as cars and radios, was so great that Japan had earned the title 'industrial superpower'.

Japan did not simply make products, she also exported them, and their quality and price made them very hard to resist. Japan's exports rose from a value of $4100 million in 1960 to a staggering $36 900 million in 1973. Japan also became a market for the products of other nations. Such countries as the United States, Saudi Arabia and Australia help to support their own economies by exporting to Japan.

---

*Using the evidence: the 'economic miracle'*

How was Japan's spectacular economic recovery achieved? The following sources provide some clues to this much-asked question.

A *. . . for the Japanese economy it [the Korean War 1950–53] was quite simply an unexpected gift. Japan, as the industrialized area nearest the war zone, was suddenly inundated with demands for vehicles, spare parts, clothing and a host of other items destined for the [mainly American] United Nations forces in Korea. . . . Between 1950 and the signing of the Korean armistice in 1953, war-related procurements in Japan are estimated to have amounted to just under one billion U.S. dollars.*

*procurements:* purchases

Tessa Morris-Suzuki: *Showa, an Inside History of Hirohito's Japan*, 1984

B *Economic recovery was assisted by United States aid. . . . Millions of dollars of aid helped to keep the economy afloat, since Japan's foreign currency earnings could hardly begin to pay for its essential imports of food and raw materials.*

Roger Buckley: *Japan Today*, 1985

C *For the building of a new Japan*
*Let's put our strength and mind together,*
*Doing our best to promote production,*
*Sending our goods to the people of the world,*
*Endlessly and continuously,*
*Like water gushing from a fountain.*
*Grow, industry, grow, grow, grow!*
*Harmony and sincerity!*
*Matsushita Electricity!*

Company song of Matsushita Electricity, sung daily by its employees. Quoted in Prue Dempster's book, *Japan Advances*, 1967

D *According to UNESCO standards, Japan's literacy rate (99.9%) is the highest in the world.*

Ardath W. Burks: *Japan, a Postindustrial Power*, 1981

E Percentage of government spending being used for defence in 1978:

| | | | |
|---|---|---|---|
| *United States* | *23%* | *Saudi Arabia* | *35.1%* |
| *West Germany* | *22.9%* | *Iran* | *23.8%* |
| *France* | *17%* | *Japan* | *5.5%* |
| *United Kingdom* | *10.5%* | *Italy* | *8.8%* |

Figures from *The Military Balance 1979–80*, published by the International Institute for Strategic Studies, London, 1980

F Savings, 1961–70. Average percentage of workers' wages which are saved:

| | | | |
|---|---|---|---|
| *Japan* | *18.6%* | *Italy* | *15.4%* |
| *West Germany* | *14.7%* | *United Kingdom* | *5.6%* |
| *France* | *12.5%* | *United States* | *6.4%* |

Figures from Hiroshi Kitamura's book, *Choices for the Japanese Economy*, 1976

G *Because a large proportion of the nation's industrial plant was destroyed or scrapped during and after the war, by the 1960s the great bulk of Japan's equipment was brand new (ten years old or less). The Japanese also made breakthroughs of their own – for example, in the use of transistors.*

Ardath W. Burks: *Japan, a Postindustrial Power*, 1981

*licence agreements:* documents giving permission to use American and European inventions

H *By means of some 5,000 licence agreements Japan has bought the most up-to-date inventions of American and European technology, while quota restrictions and high tariffs have protected her domestic producers from foreign competition.*

Richard Sims: *Modern Japan*, 1973

1 The chart on page 46 summarises the main reasons behind Japan's rapid postwar economic growth. On the chart:
a) match the source(s) with the explanation;
b) explain as fully as you can how these points might have contributed to Japan's 'economic miracle'.

An example is provided for you.

| *Reason for economic expansion* | *Source(s)* | *Contribution to the 'economic miracle'* |
| --- | --- | --- |
| Small defence budget | E | Japan spends considerably less money on defence than other world powers. The government therefore has more money available to invest in industry and the rest of the economy. |
| Attitude of workers | | |
| Korean War | | |
| Government intervention in economy | | |
| High level of savings | | |
| American aid | | |
| Quality of education | | |
| Use of latest technology | | |

2 When you have completed the chart, arrange the reasons for economic growth in order of importance, then write a paragraph justifying your choice.

## *The impact of the 'miracle'*

As Japanese exports increased after the ending of the occupation, there was scarcely a country which escaped the arrival of shiploads of goods bearing the label 'Made in Japan'. However, the success of Japan's massive export drive caused much ill-feeling among other industrialised nations. The problem was that Japan's exports were too tempting. People bought them in preference to goods produced in their own countries, with the result that the domestic industries of these countries declined. In addition to this, although Japan imported raw materials such as oil and iron ore, the country's import restrictions, imposed by the government, meant that few finished goods were allowed in. In 1968, 122 products were protected by the Japanese with import restrictions. Compared to other countries this appeared to be very unfair; West Germany, for example, protected only 43 products and Britain just 22. Japan was also accused of encouraging dubious marketing techniques, such as 'dumping':

*Japanese manufacturers of television sets are facing a major showdown with American competitors, who have accused the Japanese of dumping, i.e., selling below recognized market prices. While the Japanese TV makers firmly deny dumping, other Japanese manufacturers openly acknowledge that they often use cut-throat export prices for market penetration. To establish its air-conditioners in Western Europe, for example, Hitachi Ltd. deliberately sold below cost for three years.*

Louis Kraar: 'How the Japanese Mount That Export Blitz', *The Japan Reader*, volume 2, 1973

In the 1970s many nations, in particular the United States, began to complain angrily about Japanese trading practices. President Nixon demanded that Japan should reduce its textile exports which were having a crippling effect on the USA's southern states. Negotiations were long and bitter, but eventually Japan agreed to Nixon's demands. International pressure also forced the Japanese government to reconsider its import restrictions, and the number of products which enjoyed such protection fell to 30 by 1975.

---

### *Case study: the automobile industry*

One of the great success stories of the Japanese economy was the motor vehicle industry. In 1962, Japan could not be found among the world's top eight producers of cars. In 1979, however, Japan produced nearly ten million cars and six million motorcycles; only America produced more. In the same year, Japan's most valuable export was motor vehicles.

The rise of Japan's motor industry in the 1970s had a dramatic effect on other producers. In the first half of 1973, for example, Japan exported 44 308 cars to Britain; in the same period just 238 British cars had been sold to Japan. As Japan became the world's biggest producer of motorbikes, the British motorcycle industry found itself unable to compete and quickly collapsed. In the United States, anger and frustration at the high level of Japanese car imports was demonstrated when car workers in Detroit, America's 'motor city', began to smash the windscreens and damage the bodywork of Japanese cars. In other places, workers were forbidden to park their imported cars in company car parks.

Such protests, along with complaints from the American government, led to agreements in 1981 between Tokyo and Washington to limit the number of cars that could be exported to the United States. Japan's motor industry responded to this restriction by setting up car assembly plants overseas. Honda, for example, established a factory in the USA at Maryville, Ohio, in 1982. This was a practice that had begun in the early 1970s, when Japanese companies established factories in Taiwan, Korea, Western Europe and South America. In 1986, the car manufacturers Nissan joined an increasing number of Japanese companies operating from the north-east of England when they established an assembly plant at Washington, in Tyne and Wear.

1 Why have the Japanese been criticised sometimes for their high level of exports?

2 Make a list of all the beneficial and harmful effects of the successful Japanese economy on other countries. Arrange your work in a chart like this:

| *Beneficial effects* | *Harmful effects* |
|---|---|
| | |

## *The industrial cities*

By 1970, 75 per cent of Japan's industrial output was being produced along a 965-kilometre coastal belt of Japan's largest island, Honshu. Millions of Japanese people moved to this area, to work in the factories, shipyards and offices. By the mid-1970s, 58 per cent of

*Tokyo's business district. Compare this with the picture of Tokyo in 1945 on page 24*

*Population figures for Japan's major cities, 1983*

|  |  |
|---|---|
| Tokyo | 8 150 673 |
| Yokohama | 2 867 902 |
| Osaka | 2 535 141 |
| Nagoya | 2 058 019 |
| Kyoto | 1 460 640 |
| Sapporo | 1 450 618 |
| Kobe | 1 370 138 |
| Fukuoka | 1 081 839 |
| Kitakyushu | 1 054 531 |
| Kawasaki | 1 039 356 |

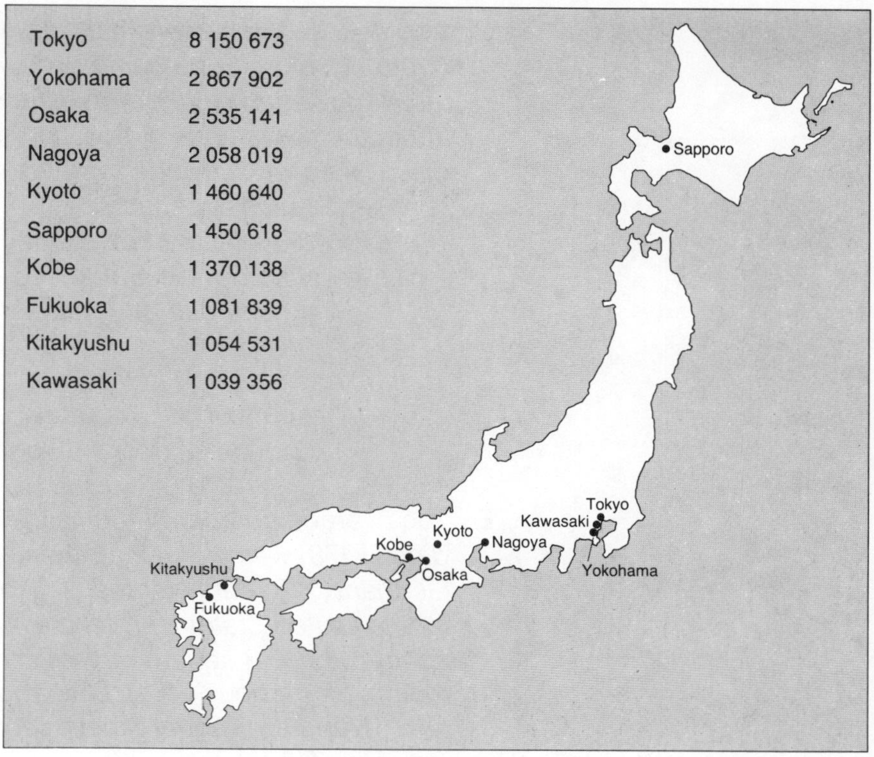


Japan's total population lived in the areas surrounding the cities of Tokyo, Osaka and Nagoya, on Honshu, and Kitakyushu on Kyushu Island in the south. In 1970 more than 18 million people lived within 50 kilometres of Tokyo's city centre. Between 1955 and 1975 Japan's major cities swelled to accommodate 37 million new citizens. The vast size of these cities, and the location of so much industry within them, caused tremendous problems for the people who lived amidst the sprawl of such urban giants.

---

### *Using the evidence: living in the city*

A *Japan has the worst problem of environmental pollution of any country in the world.*

Ui Jun: 'Pollution, Basic Theory of Kogai', *The Japan Reader*, volume 2, 1973

B *A Ministry of Construction poll conducted in September 1966 revealed that 44% of the people surveyed were dissatisfied with their present housing. . . . About half of those polled in 1966 said they found their plumbing facilities inadequate, including toilets, kitchens and baths. Another 38.6% complained about the style and structure of their dwellings. The same percentage did not like the environment, considering it inadequate for raising children.*

Masataka Kosaka: *100 Million Japanese*, 1972

C *About 40% of residents in the Tokyo–Yokohama, and Kyoto–Osaka–Kobe complexes, and slightly over 30% in the Nagoya and Northern Kyushu complexes complain about the prevalence of pollution. The ratio of residents dissatisfied with sewage systems and garbage collection services is almost identical.*

From the Asahi newspaper public opinion survey on city life, October 1965. Quoted in David John Lu's book, *Sources of Japanese History*, volume 2, 1974

D *. . . workaholics living in rabbit hutches.*

Description of Japanese city dwellers taken from a European Economic Community Report, May 1979

E *The average number of rooms per dwelling as of the same date (1978) was 4.5 (4.2 for the Federal Republic of Germany, 4.8 rooms for the United Kingdom, and 5.1 rooms for the United States), and the average size of dwelling space was 80.3 square metres compared with 79.5 square metres for France (1974), 86.0 square metres for Austria (1976), and 95.3 square metres for the Federal Republic of Germany (1976).*

Findings of the Japanese Statistics Bureau, October 1978. Quoted in *The Japan of Today*, Japanese Ministry of Foreign Affairs, 1980

F *Japanese children wearing face masks. Note the industrial complex in the background*

G *Researchers have discovered that people living in the region of the Yanagicho intersection in Shinjuku [in Tokyo] have six times the normal content of lead in their bodies. They are suffering from severe lead poisoning caused by the exhaust fumes of passing traffic. . . .*

*There have been repeated cases of schoolchildren fainting from exposure to dense photochemical smog, and of people of all ages complaining to doctors about nausea, sore eyes and hoarse throats caused by photochemical smog which combines with gases emitted from factories. . . .*

*Even worse, the very water is being poisoned by the outpourings of factories and improper sewerage facilities. It is reported that Lake Biwa is seriously polluted by human urine. . . .*

*The dreadful 'Minamata Disease' is one which is known only in Japan. . . . The water is poisoned by wastes and harmful chemicals like cyanide coming from water released by the Minamata factory of the Chisso Corporation, and by a metal-plating factory in Niigata.*

James Kirkup: *Heaven, Hell and Hara Kiri*, 1974

H

I

1 Look again at source **A**. Is this:
   a) a fact (something known to be true);
   b) an opinion (a point of view expressed without supporting evidence);
   c) a judgement (an assessment based on supporting evidence)?

2 What is meant by source **D**? Which of the other sources could you use to support the description, and what evidence could you use to show that the criticism contained in source **D** was unfair?

3 Look again at source **F**. These children are on their way to school. Why do you think they are having to wear masks over their faces?

4 Since a number of these sources were written, the Japanese have done much to ease their environmental problems. Sources **H** and **I** show two of the measures taken. Can you suggest what is happening in each of the photographs?

5 Imagine you are the secretary of an action group in one of Japan's big industrial cities in the late 1960s. Write a letter to the government, describing the problems faced by many of the citizens in your area. Try to make use of as many of the sources as possible.

*Piano-playing robot, Wabot 2, claimed to be the most talented industrial robot in the world*

## *Recent developments*

In 1971 the Japanese government set up the Environment Agency to tackle the dreadful pollution problem in Japan's industrial cities. During the following years various laws were passed which forced industry to deal with pollution hazards. In addition, compensation began to be paid to the victims of industrial pollution.

In 1973 the Arab–Israeli war seriously disrupted Japan's oil supplies. This had a considerable effect on the Japanese economy. Inflation soared to 29 per cent and growth rates fell to around five per cent. The Japanese were made painfully aware of their dependence on imports for their fuel supplies.

As a result, many Japanese companies began to turn their attention to high-technology industries which were less demanding on fuel. Japan emerged from the seventies as one of the world leaders in the production and development of computers, microchips, robotics, optical fibres and telecommunications equipment.

# 6 JAPANESE SOCIETY

Yukio Mishima

On 25 November 1970, one of Japan's best-known writers, Yukio Mishima, committed ritual suicide, or seppuku. Part of the explanation for this shocking event lay in the fact that Yukio Mishima was terribly disappointed with the way Japanese society had 'progressed' since the ending of World War II. He believed that the Japanese had become obsessed with material possessions and had largely abandoned the traditions of Japan in favour of copying the West. He was especially angered by Japan's lack of military ambition and believed that national pride in Japan's warrior past had been lost. Japanese society certainly underwent considerable changes in the postwar period, changes which Mishima simply could not accept.

## *Defence*

During the occupation Japan was given a constitution which forbade her from going to war. To some Japanese this also meant that Japan should give up her armed forces. However, as tension grew in the Far East after the ending of the Pacific War, and the forces of Communism began to move ever closer to Japan, both the American and the Japanese governments began to consider that Japan should be allowed some form of military capability. As a result in 1950 the Police Reserve Force was set up. In 1952 it was renamed the Security Force, then two years later it became the Self-Defence Force. The original Police Reserve Force was to number just 75 000. By 1979 there were almost 240 000 Japanese people in uniform, serving in the three branches of the Self-Defence Force: Air, Land and Sea. Between 1968 and 1978 the amount spent on defence in Japan rose by about 8 per cent per year; in the same period NATO defence spending increased by only 2 per cent a year. In 1979 Japan spent $10 083 million on defence, placing her sixth in the world in terms of security expenditure. Japan has certainly developed her defence capability and has come a long way since the end of the Pacific War when the intention had been to strip Japan of all military equipment and personnel.

Some important features of this military build-up must, however, be taken into account. Japan has remained committed to the idea of using her military forces for defence only; they are not to be sent abroad. This has been the position in spite of some considerable pressure from the United States to take on a more active role in international affairs. It is also true that Japan has continued to oppose nuclear weapons and every Japanese government since the

A Japanese family pose in front of the peace memorial; it carries the message 'The mistake will not be made again'

end of World War II has been careful to maintain the so-called 'three non-nuclear principles': they will not build, possess or allow nuclear weapons in Japan. The fear of nuclear weapons is so strong that the Japanese people have sometimes been described as having a 'nuclear allergy'. Certainly since the horrifying events in Hiroshima and Nagasaki in 1945, the Japanese have developed a tradition of anti-nuclear feeling. The first World Convention for the Prohibition of Atomic and Hydrogen Bombs, for example, was held in Hiroshima in 1955. Fifteen years later the determination of the Japanese to resist nuclear weapons could still be witnessed in the signing of the 1968 Nuclear Non-Proliferation Treaty, in which more than 80 nations eventually participated.

## *The crisis of 1960*

Possibly the most severe crisis in postwar Japan occurred in 1960. The Prime Minister at this time was Nobusuke Kishi, who in September 1957 had proposed a new Security Treaty with the United States. This proved to be a very unpopular move. Many Japanese people felt that it was wrong and almost certainly dangerous for Japan to continue its close association with America, especially as relations between the US and Japan's Communist neighbours were far from friendly. There was now a popular view in Japan that it was time to follow a neutral course in international affairs. In spite of popular feeling, Kishi forced the revised treaty through parliament, even resorting to having opponents of the treaty forcibly removed from the Diet building by the police. This incident outraged the Japanese people. On 20 May 1960 the revised treaty passed into law and there were angry and violent demonstrations. For several weeks the police and anti-Kishi protestors clashed in ugly street battles around the Diet building in Tokyo. An eye-witness report, broadcast on Tokyo's Radio Kanto, described one such incident on 15 June:

*night sticks:* truncheons

> *I am on top of a broadcasting car right in the middle of the demonstration. The rain is pouring down. Right in front of my eyes the police are attacking the demonstrators, beating them with night sticks. I've just been struck on the head by a policeman's club, though I am in the midst of a radio broadcast. Another is grabbing me by the neck. A policeman just shouted 'Arrest that man', pointing at me. Violence is everywhere. There is no law, no order, only hatred and anger.*
>
> Quoted in Masataka Kosaka's book, *100 Million Japanese*, 1972

The demonstration reported on Radio Kanto was colossal. One source claims that 5.8 million students and trade unionists surrounded the parliament building to voice their objections to the Kishi government. In one of the numerous violent confrontations with riot police, Miss Michiko Kamba, a young student at Tokyo University, was crushed to death in the crowd. Pressure on Kishi to resign was now irresistible and on 23 June, two days after the revised Security Treaty was approved by the Emperor, the Prime Minister announced his intention to step down. The demonstrations quickly came to an end.

## *'Income doubling'*

After the turmoil of 1960 the Japanese wished for stability, and under the new Prime Minister, Hayato Ikeda, and his successor, Eisaku Sato, they enjoyed one of the most calm and prosperous periods in recent Japanese history. On 5 September 1960, Ikeda announced his 'income doubling' proclamation, an ambitious plan to double the incomes of the Japanese people within ten years. The country became united in a massive drive to increase foreign trade and expand the economy. The plan was tremendously successful. Between 1955 and 1960 annual wage increases in Japan had totalled 5.6 per cent. This rose to 10.3 per cent during the period 1960–65.

The impact of Ikeda's plan was widely felt. For many years people in the West had regarded Japan as a country with a low standard of living. Now, with more money in their pockets, the Japanese embarked on a national spending spree which was to alter dramatically the quality of life for millions of people.

Electrical goods were the cornerstone of this consumer boom. Purchases of washing machines, refrigerators and televisions rose every year; by 1965, over 90 per cent of all Japanese households owned a television. Fashionable clothes, many of which were made from

Above: *Japanese goods on show in Hamburg in 1961. At the time, the portable television was one of the smallest models on the market*

Above right: *sport crazy – but short of space! Rooftop golfers in Tokyo*

modern synthetic fibres, became popular and gradually replaced traditional garments such as the kimono. Many Japanese people gave up using charcoal and wood for heating and cooking and switched to electricity or gas. Pre-packed and instant foods meant greater convenience and the time spent on daily chores was reduced thanks to a wide range of labour-saving electrical devices. It was even possible for families to buy their own cars, private ownership of which increased from 2.8 per cent in 1961 to 9.2 per cent in 1965. The new-found prosperity of the Japanese also led to a boom in the leisure industry. Sports such as skiing and golf were pursued enthusiastically, beaches became crowded and large-scale investment in hotels, restaurants and leisure complexes was hurriedly made in an effort to take advantage of this new interest. By 1970 the standard of living for many Japanese people had improved out of all recognition.

## *Student unrest*

The prosperity of the 1960s enabled many more young people to take advantage of higher education, and by 1978 there were over 1.8 million university students in Japan, compared to 1928 when there were only 80 900. As the student population grew, so too did their involvement in politics. They organised large-scale protests to demonstrate their opposition to such sensitive issues as the Security

*Japanese students demonstrating against anniversary celebrations for the Emperor*

Pact with the United States, nuclear power and the Vietnam War. Perhaps the most notable example of this kind of activity in recent times was the prolonged and often violent dispute over the construction of a new international airport for Tokyo built at Narita, 60 kilometres from the city centre. Work on the massive scheme began in 1970 but it was not opened until 1978, some three years behind schedule. The reason for the delay was the strength of feeling against the chosen site. About one thousand homes had to be demolished and large tracts of farmland sold to the authorities. Farmers and some local residents joined with students to make their anger felt. During the 1970s Western television frequently screened news items showing ferocious clashes between riot police and demonstrators. Casualties were sustained on both sides and there were even a number of deaths. The airport was eventually opened, but only after the authorities had taken drastic measures. One observer, Donald Mcdonald, describes what was done:

> *By erecting miles of stout metal fencing and by digging protective ditches around the airport perimeter, they rendered the site as secure as possible. Passengers entering the airport are closely scrutinised at the outer fence, and armed security agents are never far from view. It is perhaps only by being a fortress that Narita can function, but function it does.*
>
> Donald Mcdonald: *Perspectives on Japan*, volume 5, 1983

## *The position of women*

The status of women in Japan has changed considerably since the end of the occupation. In 1946 women were given the right to vote in national elections for the first time and female MPs took their seats in the Japanese parliament. In 1947 the Labour Standards Law contained the principle of equal pay for equal work, and in the law generally women were now regarded as being equal to men. Education for women became increasingly popular. In 1978 over 30 per cent of the total number of students in further education were female, a far cry from prewar days when girls were expected to wait at home until their parents found them a 'suitable' husband. The old idea of a woman's place being in the home has been steadily challenged in postwar Japan as more and more women have taken up employment, particularly in industry. By 1978 more than 20 million women were working in Japanese industry, compared with just three million in 1948. The change in attitude towards women is well illustrated by the author Masataka Kosaka:

*sake:* rice wine

> *A survey conducted in 1952 by the sociologist Takao Sofue asked for comments on a picture of a family scene. The picture showed a husband drinking sake at home while his wife and two children carried food to him on their knees. In the picture subservience to the husband was clearly depicted. The scene was actually a common one of the early days of the present century. . . . Only 19% of those who replied thought the picture showed a happy, peaceful family scene . . . 56% said the picture showed the domination of men over women, which was a feudalistic custom. Thus a change in the laws resulted in a change in attitudes.*
>
> Masataka Kosaka: *100 Million Japanese*, 1972

*Japanese women in 1956; compare the styles of dress*

*Using the evidence: changes in population*

A Growth of population in Japan:

| | |
|---|---|
| 1935 | 69.3 million |
| 1950 | 83.2 million |
| 1980 | 117 million |
| 1985 | 121 million |

B *A White Paper issued by the National Land Agency (1978) reported that there were 1,093 villages, towns and even cities (34% of all communities) that could be categorized as 'depopulated areas'. In these areas the following changes in age structure were reported:*

| *0–14 years* | *15–64 years* | *Over 65 years* |
|---|---|---|
| −20.7% | −6.1% | +9.8% |

Ardath W. Burks: *Japan, a Postindustrial Power*, 1981

C *At present (1985) about 77% of the Japanese people live in cities. Of this urban population, 59% is crowded into the 'Big Three' metropolitan areas comprising the 9 prefectures around Tokyo, Osaka and Nagoya.*

*The Japan of Today*, Japanese Ministry of Foreign Affairs, 1985

*prefectures:* units of local administration; Japan is divided into 47 prefectures

D The Japanese birth rate:

| | |
|---|---|
| 1947 | 34.3 births per thousand of the population |
| 1950s | 20.9 births per thousand (average) |
| 1960s | 17.5 births per thousand (average) |
| 1978 | 14.9 births per thousand |
| 1982 | 12.8 births per thousand |
| 1985 | 11.9 births per thousand |

The Japanese death rate:

| | |
|---|---|
| 1950s | 8.6 deaths per thousand of the population |
| 1960s | 7.1 deaths per thousand (average) |
| 1978 | 6.1 deaths per thousand |
| 1982 | 6.0 deaths per thousand |
| 1985 | 6.3 deaths per thousand |

Figures taken from *Vital Statistics*, Japanese Ministry of Health and Welfare

E *The number of medical service personnel per 1000 hospital beds increased by about 37% from 57.8 persons in 1966 to 79.1 persons in 1985. . . .*

*Medical facilities have also been increased and improved. During the past ten years [1975–85] the number of hospitals has risen by about 16% and that of hospital beds by about 28%.*

*Vital Statistics*, as above

F Percentage of total social security budget spent on pensions:

| *1965* | *1970* | *1975* | *1980* | *1985* |
|---|---|---|---|---|
| 21.9% | 24.3% | 33.3% | 42.6% | 47.7% |

1 By how much did Japan's population increase between 1935 and 1985?

2 Using the figures in source **D**, draw two graphs, one showing the Japanese birth rate from 1947 to 1985, the other showing the death rate from 1950 to 1985.
   a) Describe what has happened to both the birth rate and the death rate in Japan over this period.
   b) How would you use the figures in source **D** or the shape of your finished graphs to account for the rise in Japan's population shown in source **A**?

3 Explain how source **E** could be used to account for the changes in the Japanese death rate.
   Can you think of any other factors, not mentioned in source **E**, which would help to explain the changes in the death rate?

4 Two possible interpretations of source **F** might be that a) more money was allocated to pensions for the elderly, or b) that there are more elderly people in Japan receiving pensions. Use source **D** to decide which interpretation is more accurate.

5 What does source **B** suggest has been happening to the population of certain areas of Japan in recent years? What explanation does source **C** offer for this?

6 If you were a young person living in a rural area of Japan, how would you explain your decision to leave the village in favour of a big city? (You might find it useful to look again at the chapter on the Japanese economy.)

*Coursework assignment: Japan's foreign relations in the twentieth century*

Pupils will need to consider the numerous references to foreign affairs made throughout this book. This assignment is designed to allow pupils to concentrate on specific skills demanded by GCSE examination boards.

a) **Skill: selection, use and communication of subject content**

(i) Arrange the following events in chronological order, and provide the date of the event in brackets:

a) The attack on Pearl Harbor.
b) The invasion of Manchuria.
c) Japan's admission to the United Nations.
d) The Japanese surrender in World War II.
e) The Russo-Japanese War.
f) The signing of the San Francisco Peace and Security Treaty.

(ii) Choose two events which have been left out of this list. Write a few lines on each, explaining why you feel justified in including them in the list of significant events.

b) **Skill: understanding historical terminology and concepts**

(i) Briefly define the following terms:
a) nationalism; b) isolationism; c) disarmament.

(ii) For each of these terms provide an example from the period 1900 to 1952 to illustrate your definition.

(iii) Write about 200 words explaining how the Pacific War was caused. For the Japanese people, what were the consequences of embarking on this war?

c) **Skill: empathy**

The Japanese are sometimes criticised for failing to contribute to the general defence of the Far East. They have been seen as selfish in their determination to possess armed forces for the defence of Japan only. Write the dialogue of a debate between an American wanting to see Japan extend the role of her armed forces and a survivor of Hiroshima. Alternatively, this could be presented in role play and recorded on audio or video tape.

d) **Skill: interpretation, use and evaluation of sources**

Sources: a) Picture showing Chinese prisoners in Nanking in 1937 (page 21).
b) Picture showing Prime Minister Nakasone at the 1984 London summit meeting (page 41).

(i) What two contrasting views of Japanese foreign relations are presented in these photographs?

(ii) Photograph (a) claims to show Chinese prisoners being

bayoneted in Nanking by Japanese troops. What evidence is there in the photograph to support this claim? Suggest a possible alternative interpretation to this picture.

(iii) How could these sources be used to demonstrate the changes which Japanese foreign affairs have undergone in the twentieth century?

(iv) To what extent would you agree with the view that photographs such as these are inadequate as sources of information for the historian who wishes to make judgements about the past?

---

# Skills grid

*Key*
**U** Using the evidence
**Q** Questions
**C** Coursework assignment

## A Historical skills

| | U | U | Q | Q | Q | U | Q | Q | Q | U | Q | Q | Q | Q | Q | Q | Q | Q | Q | Q | Q | Q | Q | Q | C |
|---|---|---|---|---|---|---|---|---|---|---|---|---|---|---|---|---|---|---|---|---|---|---|---|---|---|
| | 7 | 10 | 11 | 12 | 16 | 21 | 22 | 25 | 27 | 29 | 32 | 34 | 37 | 41 | 42 | 43 | 45 | 47 | 48 | 50 | 51 | 55 | 57 | 60 | 61 |
| **1 *Using historical evidence*** | | | | | | | | | | | | | | | | | | | | | | | | | |
| Comprehension of variety of sources | ■ | | | | | | | | | | | | | | | | | | | | | | | | |
| Listing primary and secondary sources | | | | | | ■ | | | | | | | | | | | | | | | | | | | |
| Extraction of information | ■ | ■ | | | ■ | ■ | | | ■ | ■ | ■ | | | | ■ | ■ | | | | ■ | ■ | ■ | | ■ | ■ |
| Evaluation, recognising * fact *v* opinion | | | ■ | | | | | | | | | | | | | | | | | | | | | | |
| * gaps and inconsistencies | ■ | | | | | | | | | | | | | | | | | | | | | | | | |
| * bias | | ■ | | | | ■ | | | | ■ | | | | | | | | | ■ | | | | ■ | | |
| * importance of origin and context | | | | | | ■ | ■ | | | | | | | | | | | | | | | | | | ■ |
| Recognition of inference and implication in a source | ■ | | | | | | | | | | ■ | | | | | | | | | | | ■ | ■ | | |
| Comparison of different sources based on relative reliability | | ■ | | | | ■ | ■ | ■ | ■ | | | | | | | | | | | | | | | | ■ |
| Reaching conclusions on basis of this comparison | | | | | | | ■ | ■ | ■ | | | | | | | | | | | | | | | ■ | ■ |
| Judgement and choice between various opinions | ■ | | | | | ■ | | ■ | | ■ | | | | | | | | | | | | | | | ■ |
| Formation of overview and synthesis of one's own opinion | ■ | | | ■ | ■ | | | | | | ■ | | | | ■ | | ■ | | | | ■ | ■ | | | ■ |
| **2 *Empathy*** | | | | | | | | | | | | | | | | | | | | | | | | | |
| Understanding events and issues from perspective of people in the past | | | | | | | | ■ | | | | | ■ | ■ | | | ■ | ■ | ■ | | | ■ | ■ | ■ | ■ |

## B Historical concepts

| | 7 | 10 | 11 | 12 | 16 | 21 | 22 | 25 | 27 | 29 | 32 | 34 | 37 | 41 | 42 | 43 | 45 | 47 | 48 | 50 | 51 | 55 | 57 | 60 | 61 |
|---|---|---|---|---|---|---|---|---|---|---|---|---|---|---|---|---|---|---|---|---|---|---|---|---|---|
| Cause and consequence | | ■ | | | ■ | | | | | | ■ | | | | ■ | | | ■ | | | ■ | ■ | | | |
| Continuity and change | | | | | | | | | | | | ■ | | | | | ■ | | | | | | | | ■ |
| Similarity and difference | | ■ | | | ■ | ■ | ■ | ■ | ■ | | | ■ | | | | | | | | | | | | | ■ |
| Time, sequence and chronology | | | | | | | | | | | | ■ | | | | | | | | | | | | | |
| Conflict and consensus | | | | | | | | | | | ■ | ■ | | | | | | | | | | ■ | ■ | | |
| Historical vocabulary and terminology | | ■ | ■ | | ■ | | ■ | | | | | | | | | ■ | | | | | | | | | ■ |
| Key concepts | ■ | | | | ■ | | | | | | | | | | | | | | | | | | | | |

# INDEX